INTRODUCING ISSUES WITH

OPPOSING VIEWPOINTS®

GENETIC ENGINEERING

Other books in the Introducing Issues
with Opposing Viewpoints series:

AIDS
Alcohol
Civil Liberties
Cloning
The Death Penalty
Gangs
Gay Marriage
Smoking
Terrorism

INTRODUCING ISSUES WITH

OPPOSING VIEWPOINTS®

GENETIC ENGINEERING

Scott Barbour, *Book Editor*

Bruce Glassman, *Vice President*
Bonnie Szumski, *Publisher, Series Editor*
Helen Cothran, *Managing Editor*

OPPOSING VIEWPOINTS® SERIES

GREENHAVEN PRESS
An imprint of Thomson Gale, a part of The Thomson Corporation

THOMSON

GALE

Detroit • New York • San Francisco • San Diego • New Haven, Conn. • Waterville, Maine • London • Munich

LIBRARY OF CONGRESS CATALOGING-IN-PUBLICATION DATA

Genetic engineering / Scott Barbour, book editor.
   p. cm. — (Introducing issues with opposing viewpoints)
   Includes bibliographical references and index.
   ISBN 0-7377-3223-7 (lib. : alk. paper)
   1. Genetic engineering—Social aspects. 2. Genetic engineering—Moral and ethical aspects. I. Barbour, Scott, 1963– II. Series.
   QH438.7.G412 2006
   306.4'6—dc22
                                                    2005050210

Printed in the United States of America

CONTENTS

FOREWORD

Indulging in a wide spectrum of ideas, beliefs, and perspectives is a critical cornerstone of democracy. After all, it is often debates over differences of opinion, such as whether to legalize abortion, how to treat prisoners, or when to enact the death penalty that shape our society and drive it forward. Such diversity of thought is frequently regarded as the hallmark of a healthy and civilized culture. As the Reverend Clifford Schutjer of the First Congregational Church in Mansfield, Ohio, declared in a 2001 sermon, "Surrounding oneself with only like-minded people, restricting what we listen to or read only to what we find agreeable is irresponsible. Refusing to entertain doubts once we make up our minds is a subtle but deadly form of arrogance." With this advice in mind, Introducing Issues with Opposing Viewpoints books aim to open readers' minds to the critically divergent views that comprise our world's most important debates.

Introducing Issues with Opposing Viewpoints simplifies for students the enormous and often overwhelming mass of material now available via print and electronic media. Collected in every volume is an array of opinions that capture the essence of a particular controversy or topic. Introducing Issues with Opposing Viewpoints books embody the spirit of nineteenth-century journalist Charles A. Dana's axiom: "Fight for your opinions, but do not believe that they contain the whole truth, or the only truth." Absorbing such contrasting opinions teaches students to analyze the strength of an argument and compare it to its opposition. From this process readers can inform and strengthen their own opinions, or be exposed to new information that will change their minds. Introducing Issues with Opposing Viewpoints is a mosaic of different voices. The authors are statesmen, pundits, academics, journalists, corporations, and ordinary people who have felt compelled to share their experiences and ideas in a public forum. Their words have been collected from newspapers, journals, books, speeches, interviews, and the Internet, the fastest growing body of opinionated material in the world.

Introducing Issues with Opposing Viewpoints shares many of the well-known features of its critically acclaimed parent series, Opposing Viewpoints. The articles are presented in a pro/con format, allowing readers to absorb divergent perspectives side by side. Active reading questions preface each viewpoint, requiring the student to approach the material thoughtfully and carefully. Useful charts, graphs, and cartoons supplement each article. A thorough introduction provides readers with crucial background on an issue. An annotated bibliography points the reader toward articles, books, and Web sites that contain additional information on the topic. An appendix of organizations to contact contains a wide variety of charities, nonprofit organizations, political groups, and private enterprises that each hold a position on the issue at hand. Finally, a comprehensive index allows readers to locate content quickly and efficiently.

Introducing Issues with Opposing Viewpoints is also significantly different from Opposing Viewpoints. As the series title implies, its presentation will help introduce students to the concept of opposing viewpoints, and learn to use this material to aid in critical writing and debate. The series' four-color, accessible format makes the books attractive and inviting to readers of all levels. In addition, each viewpoint has been carefully edited to maximize a reader's understanding of the content. Short but thorough viewpoints capture the essence of an argument. A substantial, thought-provoking essay question placed at the end of each viewpoint asks the student to further investigate the issues raised in the viewpoint, compare and contrast two authors' arguments, or consider how one might go about forming an opinion on the topic at hand. Each viewpoint contains sidebars that include at-a-glance information and handy statistics. A Facts About section located in the back of the book further supplies students with relevant facts and figures.

Following in the tradition of the Opposing Viewpoints series, Greenhaven Press continues to provide readers with invaluable exposure to the controversial issues that shape our world. As John Stuart Mill once wrote: "The only way in which a human being can make some approach to knowing the whole of a subject is by hearing what can be said about it by persons of every variety of opinion and studying all modes in which it can be looked at by every character of mind. No wise man ever acquired his wisdom in any mode but this." It is to this principle that Introducing Issues with Opposing Viewpoints books are dedicated.

INTRODUCTION

"By responsible use of science, technology, and other rational means we shall eventually manage to become post-human, beings with vastly greater capacities than present human beings have."

—philosopher Nick Bostrom

The term *genetic engineering* refers to the science of moving and altering genes in order to change the traits of living organisms. This science is applied to plants, animals, and humans. In agriculture, new genes are introduced into plants for a variety of reasons, such as to make them stronger, less vulnerable to pests, and more productive. Similarly, new genes are transferred into animals in order, for example, to create cows that produce more milk or goats that produce milk that contains proteins for medical treatments.

Because these uses of genetic technology involve moving genes from one organism to another—and even from one species to another—they are highly controversial. For example, debate rages over whether genetically altered crops pose threats to the environment or human health, whether foods that contain genetically modified ingredients should be labeled, and whether the genetic engineering of animals is ethical. Although the genetic engineering of plants and animals is a contentious issue, the application of genetic engineering technology to humans is perhaps even more divisive.

There are two types of human genetic engineering: somatic gene therapy and germ line engineering. Somatic gene therapy involves altering a patient's somatic, or body, cells in order to treat a genetic disorder. This form of genetic engineering is generally free of controversy because only the person being treated is affected by the procedure; the changes it makes are not transmitted to the patient's offspring. Germ line engineering, on the other hand, involves altering the genetic make-up of sperm or egg cells. Because these are reproductive cells, the changes that are made to them are passed on to all succeeding generations. Thus germ line engineering, which is also known as inheritable genetic modification, makes irreversible changes to the human genetic legacy.

A scientist conducts genetic research in a lab. Some researchers hope to use genetic engineering to treat diseases and enhance human abilities.

Although this technology has yet to be applied to humans, it has been used on animals; scientists believe it is only a matter of time before engineering of the human germ line becomes a reality.

The prospect of using germ line engineering to treat genetic diseases attracts little criticism. After all, the idea that parents might be able to ensure that their children are free of a genetic illness is exciting. And the idea that they might be able to go a step further and ensure that not only their children, but their grandchildren, great-grandchildren, and all subsequent generations will be free of the illness is equally appealing. The possibility that society could rid itself entirely of certain genetic illnesses is one of the greatest promises that genetic engineering technology offers.

However, some proponents of the technology advocate going beyond curing diseases. They advocate using the technology for "genetic enhancement"—that is, to improve human beings. Typically, these proponents look forward to a day, perhaps in the next generation or so, when parents will be able to use genetic engineering to create "designer babies"—offspring that are not only free of disease, but that possess traits that are deemed desirable by the parents or by society in general. For example, parents may choose to create a child who has a particular hair color, who is especially intelligent and athletic, or who has a creative personality. As stated by Lee Silver, a biologist and the author of *Remaking Eden: Cloning and Beyond in a Brave New World,* "Parents are going to be able to give their children genes that other children get naturally, such as genes that increase athletic ability, genes that increase musical talents . . . and, ultimately, genes that affect cognitive abilities."

Creating a Post-Human Species

Lee and others argue that as more and more parents avail themselves of this technology, germ line engineering will have a profound impact on society and indeed the human race. They contend that genetic engineering could move the human race to a new stage of evolution— in other words, to the development of a post-human species. As Gregory Stock, director of the Program on Medicine, Technology, and Society at UCLA's School of Medicine, states, "Well before this new millennium's close, we will almost certainly change ourselves enough to become much more than simply human." Advocates of genetic enhancement predict that this species will be vastly more intelligent than humans, will be capable of living hundreds or thousands of years, if not indefinitely, and will be free of the diseases that currently plague humans. Due to their superiority, they will create a society free of war, violent crime, addiction, poverty, and other human problems.

Other predictions of the post-human future are less rosy. Because genetic enhancement is likely to be expensive, only the wealthy will be able to afford it. Thus it is possible that not all humans will evolve to the next level. Lee Silver, although he advocates human germ line engineering, describes a future society consisting of the "gen-rich" (people who are genetically enhanced) and the "naturals" (people who are not genetically enhanced). He envisions the divide between the two groups growing until they are two different species that no longer breed with each other. The gen-rich may then discriminate against the naturals. "I think it's going to be a disaster because one group of people who is a different species to the other group of people will no longer have the desire or need to treat that second group of people with dignity and respect."

Maxwell J. Mehlman, a professor of law and bioethics and the author of *Wondergenes: Genetic Enhancement and the Future of Society,* takes this idea of a society divided into two species a step further. He sug-

Genetic engineering could someday be used to improve people's athleticism.

A scientist examines genetic information. Researchers can use such knowledge to screen people for genetic disorders.

gests that the enhanced group may evolve into "a race of highly intelligent, genetically enhanced monsters." He asks,

> What if instead of just increasing height by several inches, genetic enhancement increased it by several feet? If someone could lift, not just a few hundred additional pounds, but a few thousand? If instead of being boosted by a score of IQ points, brainpower exceeded the capabilities of the fastest computers?

If this scenario comes to pass, Mehlman fears, the enhanced species could subject the unenhanced species to cruel treatment:

> As the members of the superior race look down on the unenhanced, they may decide that the unenhanced, while clever little creatures, do not deserve the same civil and political rights. Driven

by disregard or contempt for their unenhanced forebears, the superior species may become callous, malevolent slave-masters. They may even decide that they have no further use for the unenhanced. Except perhaps to toy with them.

Although this prediction seems fanciful, it illustrates, in a somewhat exaggerated form, one of the major concerns of those who oppose the use of germ line therapy to enhance human beings or to move the human race to the next stage of evolution.

The application of germ line therapy to human beings is decades away. For now, all of the debate over the prospect of designer babies, genetic enhancement, and a post-human species is speculative and theoretical. It is likely that, as with most technologies, the genetic engineering of humans will bring changes that are less dramatic than proponents hope for and less harmful than critics fear. The topic of human enhancement is among the issues debated in *Introducing Issues with Opposing Viewpoints: Genetic Engineering,* which contains the following chapters: Should Genetic Engineering Be Used to Improve Human Beings? and Is the Genetic Engineering of Plants and Animals Beneficial? In these chapters, authors debate the impact of genetic engineering technology on the environment, human health, and society. As the science continues to develop, these debates are sure to grow more intense and to occupy a more central place in people's lives.

CHAPTER 1

Should Genetic Engineering Be Used to Improve Human Beings?

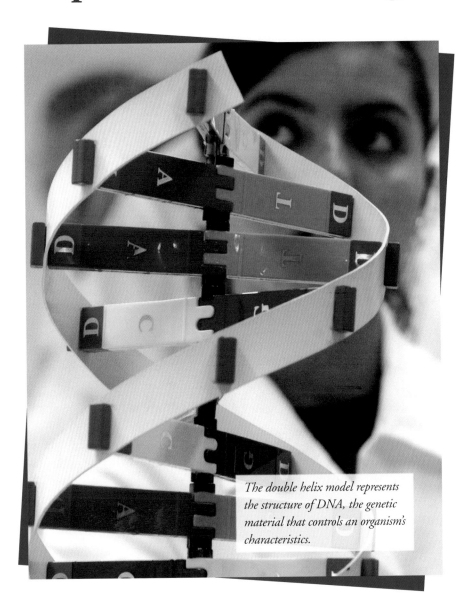

The double helix model represents the structure of DNA, the genetic material that controls an organism's characteristics.

Genetic Engineering Should Be Used to Improve Human Beings

Gregory Stock, interviewed by Erika Jonietz

"When medical science begins to understand genetics, it will become possible to screen for various constellations of genes that will likely bring beneficial effects."

Gregory Stock is the director of the Program on Medicine, Technology, and Society at the University of California, Los Angeles. He is also the author of the book *Redesigning Ourselves: Our Inevitable Genetic Futures* and is well known as an advocate of using genetic engineering technology to improve human beings by controlling their physical, mental, and psychological characteristics. In the following viewpoint, Stock is interviewed by Erica Jonietz of *Technology Review* magazine. In the interview, Stock contends that within one generation, emerging genetic technologies will allow parents to control the genetic makeup of their children. This process will permit them not only to prevent diseases but also to choose desirable traits in their offspring. Although scientists are not yet sure exactly what choices will be possible, Stock acknowledges, dramatic changes in the way that humans reproduce are inevitable due to the rapid development of genetic science.

AS YOU READ, CONSIDER THE FOLLOWING QUESTIONS:
1. What existing reproductive technology does Stock compare to genetic engineering?
2. What traits does Stock believe parents will be able to engineer in their children?
3. According to Stock, why do opponents want to stop human genetic engineering?

Technology Review: You claim that parents will be able to genetically enhance their unborn children. But how realistic is the idea of genetically engineering embryos, eggs, or sperm—our "germline cells"—to create designer babies? It sounds like science fiction.

Gregory Stock: For the immediate future, it is. You have to have two things first: something worth doing and a safe, reliable way of doing it. At present, neither exists. There really are no platforms for doing reliable, safe interventions of this sort. And even if you had a safe way of inserting genes, you wouldn't have anything to do, because we don't know enough about our genetics to accomplish anything that would be worth whatever risks are involved.

But that doesn't mean that such modifications are particularly distant. Both those requirements, I expect, will be met within the next generation, so it's good to start thinking about these sorts of things now. The potentials will arrive quickly once the technology moves forward.

Making Choices About Children

TR: In what ways are people already starting to confront the ethical issues associated with choosing children's genetic fates?

Stock: We are beginning to open up our biology and intervene in realms that have always been beyond our reach. Well before the technology of germline intervention itself is ready for prime time, we'll be dealing with sophisticated screening that allows prospective parents to use genetic tests to pick and choose among their embryos. Preimplantation genetic screening already has been used with in vitro fertilization for a decade to avoid serious genetic diseases like cystic fibrosis. Parents test their embryos for the mutation and discard those that are afflicted. Soon, such testing will move to a broad array of potential genetic diseases, then to lesser vulnerabilities like a heightened risk for severe depression, and then to nondisease traits—choices about temperament and personality.

The controversies provoked by these capabilities and how parents use them will be very similar to the ones we will face in manipulating the germline directly. Functionally, there's little distinction between going in and modifying a gene to correct a mutation that will cause Huntington's disease and simply screening to avoid that mutation; or between picking an embryo with certain potentials and adding genes to create them. So I see this as a broad policy debate that is less about a particular technology than about the capacity for parents to make choices about the genetics of their children.

TR: What kinds of traits will it be possible to engineer? Are parents going to be able to pick the height, intelligence, or musical talents of their children?

Advocates of genetic enhancement hope that parents of the future will be able to alter the DNA of embryos to produce children with favorable traits.

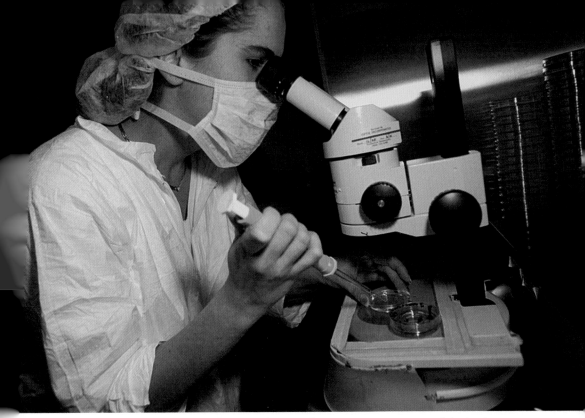

An embryologist examines frozen embryos under a microscope as part of the in vitro fertilization process.

Stock: Right now we don't know what's going to be too complicated to do and what will be very, very easy. I think we'll be surprised at the numbers of things that turn out to be easy. Certainly, there have already been complex traits—ones undoubtedly shaped by many genes—that can be substantively altered by changing one gene. Researchers have modified single genes to roughly double the life span of fruit flies and roundworms. And there was recently an astonishing study where researchers changed one gene in mice, and it greatly enlarged their brains and gave them a wrinkled, deeply folded surface similar to that of the human brain instead of the smoothness typical of a mouse. When medical science begins to understand our genetics, it will become possible to screen for various constellations of genes that will likely bring beneficial effects—tendencies towards vitality and health or various personalities and predispositions we like. And once we start using such information to choose embryos, it won't take us long to start thinking seriously about just going in and creating those sorts of genetic constellations directly.

Unstoppable Technology

TR: You speak of "our inevitable genetic future." Won't numerous groups want to limit if not outright ban such technology?

Stock: No matter how much we discuss these things, we're not going to reach a consensus about what should be done. These issues touch our values too deeply, hinging on culture, religion, and philosophy. Those who want to stop such technology do not want to do so because they

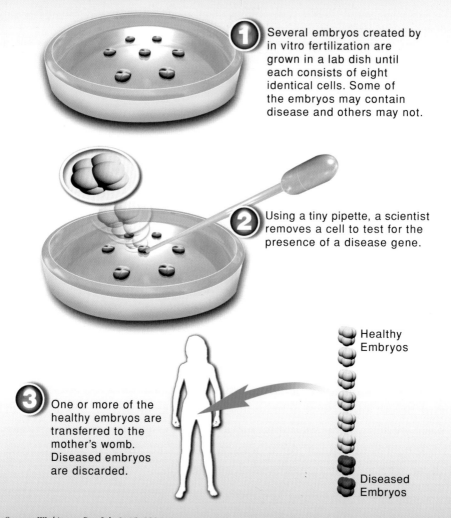

Screening Out Genetic Disease

After in vitro fertilization, geneticists can test embryos for disease-causing genes before they are transferred into a mother's womb.

1 Several embryos created by in vitro fertilization are grown in a lab dish until each consists of eight identical cells. Some of the embryos may contain disease and others may not.

2 Using a tiny pipette, a scientist removes a cell to test for the presence of a disease gene.

3 One or more of the healthy embryos are transferred to the mother's womb. Diseased embryos are discarded.

Healthy Embryos

Diseased Embryos

Source: *Washington Post,* July 9–15, 2001.

think it may go awry and cause injuries, although that's what they say. They want to stop it because they fear it will be wildly successful and sweep humanity toward a pernicious future. And they feel an urgency to stop such technology now, before it even arrives, because they're afraid that if we get too much benefit from it, then too many people will see it as desirable. For example, you would be hard put to ban in vitro fertilization now: too many children are here because of the technology; too many happy parents would be childless without it. And it could be the same with many of these other technologies.

I don't believe it will be possible to stop germline intervention. But the politics will have impacts on where breakthroughs are made. A good example is therapeutic cloning—the work on embryonic stem cells to treat Alzheimer's, diabetes, and other diseases. Even though the 2002 attempt to ban this in the United States failed, the associated uncertainty has made this country a very problematic environment for doing this sort of work. So a number of researchers have moved overseas: there are strong efforts in Britain, Singapore, and Australia. The U.S. government could not halt these technologies, even if it wanted to. We can make a lot of noise about particular clinical applications, but ultimately we should remember that this will happen because these potentials are really just spinoffs of mainstream medical research that we all want.

> ## FAST FACT
>
> A germ line is the cellular lineage of any organism that reproduces sexually. Germ line engineering would involve altering the genetic makeup of this cellular lineage. These changes to the germ line would be permanent and irreversible and would be passed on to all future generations. Scientists have not yet attempted germ line engineering, which is also called germ line therapy and inheritable genetic modification.

A Biological Divide?

TR: Creating designer babies seems like a procedure that, at least for a while, will be restricted to the wealthy. Will this be a biological equivalent of the digital divide?

Stock: All these technologies tend to be available initially to the more affluent and more motivated. That's the way it works with every technology. In vitro fertilization was enormously expensive a decade and a half ago. And now, it's come down to where a person can go through an IVF procedure for $6,000 to $8,000, which is not inexpensive but is certainly well within the means of a vast number of families in this country. There are about 25,000 kids born by IVF in the U.S. every year. And if you compare it with the cost of a car, it's affordable.

These early users do us a great service. They test these technologies for us and even pay enormous sums for the privilege. In a way, they function as guinea pigs for the rest of humanity. If you had to think of who you'd like to test these technologies, what better group can you imagine? They're well informed, highly motivated, eager, hard to coerce, and they are definitely volunteers.

I think the biggest gulfs will not be between the rich and the poor of one generation, but between one generation and the next generation and the next generation after that. This is because what is available today is so very primitive compared to what will be available 25 years from now, and that too will seem primitive after yet a further 25 years.

EVALUATING THE AUTHORS' ARGUMENTS:

In the article you just read, Gregory Stock describes some of the choices parents may be able to make about the traits of their future children. In the next viewpoint, Mark S. Frankel also discusses the possible choices that genetic engineering may offer parents. Do you think parents should have this type of control over the characteristics of their offspring? Why or why not?

Genetic Engineering Should Not Be Used to Improve Human Beings

Mark S. Frankel

"No IGM [inheritable genetic modification] ... should go forward at this time."

In the following viewpoint Mark S. Frankel calls for a cautious approach to applying genetic engineering technology to human beings. He specifically opposes making inheritable genetic modifications (IGMs)—that is, genetic changes that will be passed on to future generations. Using this technology to prevent genetic diseases is unnecessary, he argues, since less drastic options are available to prevent the transmission of such illnesses to offspring. He also rejects the idea of using IGM to enhance human beings by controlling their intelligence, eye color, or other traits. The outcome of such efforts is too unpredictable to be allowed at this time. Mark S. Frankel is director of the Program on Scientific Freedom, Responsibility, and Law at the American Association for the Advancement of Science, a nonprofit organization dedicated to promoting science.

Mark S. Frankel, "Inheritable Genetic Modification and a Brave New World," *Hastings Center Report*, vol. 33, March/April 2003. Copyright © 2003 by the Hastings Center. Reproduced by permission.

AS YOU READ, CONSIDER THE FOLLOWING QUESTIONS:
1. What techniques already exist to avoid passing mutant genes on to children, as explained by Frankel?
2. How might the use of genetic enhancement technology change people's view of human development, according to the author?
3. Why does the author believe that the idea of using genetic engineering for enhancement might become more acceptable?

I n the fall of 2000, the American Association for the Advancement of Science called on science to slow down. In a report it issued on inheritable genetic modification, AAAS took the position that no genetic modifications affecting the germ line, whether intentional or inadvertent, should be undertaken until the technology's safety, efficacy, and social implications had been subject to widespread public discussion. Further, said AAAS, there should be no work on inheritable genetic modification until a system of public oversight was in place that exercised authority over research in both the public and private sectors. . . .

By inheritable genetic modification, or IGM, I mean interventions capable of modifying genes that are transmitted to offspring and to generations beyond. . . . Although we have much to learn about applying IGM techniques to humans, researchers have established proof of principle in animals, where foreign genes introduced into mice have been transmitted and expressed for at least three generations. Moreover, recent advances in stem cell and cloning research, which were reported after completion of the AAAS study, will likely provide more options for doing IGM. As knowledge of human genetics grows in the years ahead, the technical obstacles may fall by the wayside sooner than we expect. To what uses, then, might IGM be put? One would be to target IGM toward the alleviation or elimination of genetic diseases. The other would be to enhance human traits.

The Promise of Health
In principle, IGM would have the benefit of preventing the inheritance of genetic diseases in families rather than treating it every time it appears, generation after generation. And by targeting either germ

cells or the embryo, IGM could intervene before a condition occurs—before it causes irreversible damage. . . .

There already exist, however, other, better-tested techniques to avoid passing on mutant genes. These include genetic screening and counseling; prenatal diagnosis and abortion, egg or sperm donation, and adoption either of a child or an embryo. Another technique, known as pre-implantation genetic diagnosis, combines in vitro fertilization (IVF) with pre-implantation diagnosis and selection of embryos. Individual cells are removed from an embryo, fertilized outside the body, and tested for the presence of genetic mutations (to the extent that tests are available). Embryos without known mutations are then implanted in the woman via IVF. This approach could have wide application, although it would not work in those cases where both parents have identical versions of the same mutant gene.

A pregnant woman undergoes an ultrasound, which can detect if there are bodily abnormalities in her unborn fetus.

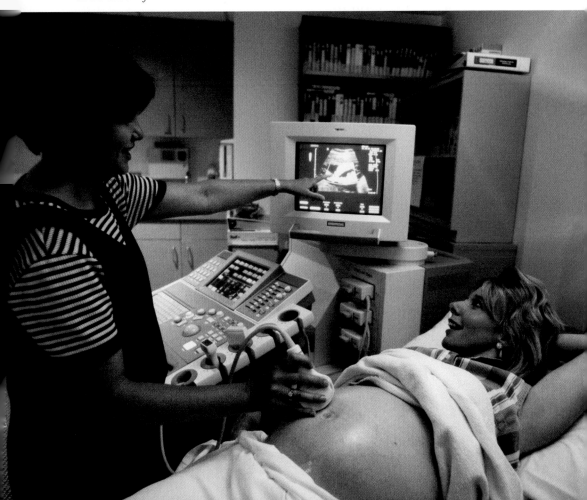

With these techniques available, and in light of the enormous difficulties associated with determining risks, why bother with IGM? The answer lies in its possible use for genetic enhancement.

Pursuing Enhancement

It is this prospect, I believe, that generates the most excitement over IGM, and the most uneasiness. . . .

By "genetic enhancement" I mean improving human traits that without intervention would be within the range of what is commonly regarded as normal, or improving them beyond what is needed to maintain or restore good health. Examples could include increasing height, improving intelligence, altering behavior, or changing eye color, all of which have been shown to have some underlying genetic connection. IGM offers the promise that genes associated with characteristics found to be undesirable (or less desirable) could be replaced by those linked to desired traits.

Genetic engineering may someday allow parents to choose their baby's eye color.

There are promises and perils associated with genetic enhancement. On the one hand, we know that some people are born more "genetically fit" than others, giving them certain advantages. The promise of enhancing the capabilities of those who are genetically less fortunate is an exciting and noble prospect for some people. And by increasing, for example, the intelligence of individuals, all of society may gain from the knowledge they generate.

On the other hand, genetic enhancement could also lead us to devalue various social and environmental factors that influence human development in concert with genes. There might be less appreciation for productive social interaction in a classroom, for example, or for the hard work traditionally required to become a successful professional. These conventional methods of enhancement may have some intrinsic value that could never be duplicated by a genetic intervention. In fact, a preoccupation with genetic enhancement may place too much emphasis on the genes and ultimately prevent us from solving problems that are really embedded in the structure of our society.

FAST FACT

In a 2002 poll conducted by the Discovery Channel, 87 percent of Americans opposed allowing parents to use genetic engineering to "design" a baby to satisfy their personal, cultural, or aesthetic desires. Ninety-two percent of British respondents opposed this use of genetic technology.

Perils

Another complication is that the technology developed for therapeutic purposes will be the same as that used for enhancement. So while we might approve of IGM for medical treatment, its availability will likely promote creeping enhancement applications as well. For example, scientists are now testing the use of gene transfer to strengthen the muscles of children with muscular dystrophy, but the same technique could be used to increase an athlete's strength and endurance. An even more revealing example concerns the use of Human Growth Hormone, or HGH, which is genetically engineered to supplement natural growth hormone. While originally approved to treat children deficient in natural growth

Source: Rick McKee. © 2002 by *The Augusta Chronicle*. Reproduced by permission.

hormone, it could be used to make normal children taller, and indeed one newspaper has reported that some parents have requested HGH for children within the normal height range for their age because they want to improve their chances in competitive basketball.

Further complicating matters is that distinguishing between treatment and enhancement may get increasingly difficult. The line where one ends and the other begins may become blurred as our experience with IGM expands. Hence, interventions which now give us pause may become more acceptable in the future. Surveys have shown that 40 to 45 percent of Americans approve of using genetic technologies to bolster their children's physical and mental traits. I suspect that as more people get used to the idea, it will become even more appealing. Americans already avail themselves of cosmetic surgery to make them look better, drugs to make them more alert, and herbs to promote sexual performance. And we expect and praise parents for doing all that they can to enhance their children's well-being. . . . For many Americans, IGM will merely be seen as a logical extension of what is commonplace throughout America today, and it will be increasingly difficult to draw a clear line between the use of genetics for therapeutic purposes and its use for other ends.

Yet enhancement by genetics is also qualitatively different from enhancement by other means. Existing methods of enhancement, from pharmacology to advanced music lessons, are aimed at the current generation of adults and children. They are not biologically intrusive in a manner that will significantly shape our evolutionary course. Inheritable genetic enhancement would have long-term effects on persons yet to be born. Thus we have little, if any, precedent for this way of using IGM. We would be venturing into unknown territory, but without any sense of where the boundaries should lie, much less with an understanding of what it means to cross such boundaries. . . .

So what do we do? The 2000 AAAS report recommended several steps that remain important. Most important among them was that no IGM, whether involving intentional or "reasonably foreseeable" inadvertent transmission, should go forward at this time. In a subsequent article appearing in *Science* . . . , my coauthor and I stressed the urgency of moving more quickly to put in place a system of public oversight with authority over IGM efforts in both the public and private sectors. Accompanying this oversight mechanism should be a national public dialogue on whether and, if it is deemed acceptable, how such research and its applications should proceed.

These proposals are premised not on a belief that IGM should never be tried, but that it must pass the test of public discourse, undergo rigorous assessment of its potential impacts, and receive explicit public approval. There should be no backdoors, whether due to gaps in public policy or an aggressive marketplace, through which IGM inches its way into our lives. These technologies are highly seductive, and we could easily get used to them without fully considering their consequences.

EVALUATING THE CARTOON:

Analyze the cartoon on page 28 of this viewpoint. Is this cartoon funny? If so, what makes it humorous? Do you think the cartoonist is making a serious point? If so, what point is being made?

Human Genetic Enhancement Would Be Unethical

"Changing a future child's genetic makeup, and experimenting with the genetic legacy of humanity, fall outside any acceptable notion of individual rights or parental prerogatives."

Marcy Darnovsky

In the following viewpoint Marcy Darnovsky presents ethical arguments against using genetic engineering to cure diseases or enhance human beings. She contends that using genetic enhancement technology would undermine the value of human life, encourage discrimination against the disabled, and erode the community's commitment to improving society in traditional ways. Contrary to the arguments of proponents, Darnovsky argues that parents and researchers do not have the right to employ genetic technology without the sanction of society at large. Marcy Darnovsky is the associate executive director of the Center for Genetics and Society, a nonprofit organization that encourages responsible uses and effective governance of human genetic and reproductive technologies.

Marcy Darnovsky, "Embryo Cloning and Beyond," *Tikkun*, vol. 17, July/August 2002. Copyright © 2002 by the Institute for Labor and Mental Health. Reproduced by permission of *Tikkun:* A Bimonthly Jewish Critique of Politics, Culture & Society.

AS YOU READ, CONSIDER THE FOLLOWING QUESTIONS:
1. How does biologist Lee Silver describe the future that will result from genetic and reproductive technologies, as summarized by the author?
2. Why is inheritable genetic modification unnecessary in order to prevent disease, according to Darnovsky?
3. How does the author respond to the argument that genetic enhancement is simply a reproductive choice?

I began paying attention to . . . questions [about genetic technologies] several years ago, after reading Princeton molecular biologist Lee Silver's notorious account of the new human genetic and reproductive technologies in his book, *Remaking Eden: Cloning and Beyond in a Brave New World.* Silver enthusiastically predicts that well-off parents will one day soon choose their children's DNA from a biotech catalog. This new market-based mode of childbearing is inevitable, he says, and will lead to the emergence first of genetic castes, which he dubs the "GenRich" and the "Naturals," and thereafter of separate human species.

At first I assumed that Silver was merely indulging in a bit of mad-scientist headline grabbing. When I learned that his vision of a "posthuman" future is shared—and being publicly promoted—by a disturbing number of other mainstream scientists, bioethicists, pundits, and biotech entrepreneurs, I began to look for the progressive response. I expected some combination of alarm, sharp analysis, outrage, and ridicule. I found all that, but far less of it than I'd expected. Meanwhile, new genetic and reproductive technologies were burgeoning, biotech startups were raking in investment capital, and an extreme techno-libertarian ideology was taking root.

Before long, however, a growing network of progressives—scholars, scientists, advocates of environmental protection, women's health, human rights, disability rights, civil rights, and indigenous rights—did begin to mobilize around the threat of the new techno-eugenics. Our work had just gotten underway when the controversy about embryo cloning erupted, forcing us to engage a divisive issue of secondary concern rather than remaining focused on a unifying issue of primary concern. . . .

The Technology of Eugenic Engineering

In all the commentary about human cloning, few have noticed the most significant threat it poses: Embryo cloning is the technology that would make the creation of eugenically engineered "designer babies" commercially feasible.

The process of producing a genetically redesigned child would involve creating an embryo through in vitro fertilization, culturing ES [embryonic stem] cells derived from it to provide a sufficient population for the tricky task of inserting the desired genes, and then extracting the nucleus of a successfully altered stem cell to construct a cloned embryo. The resulting child would not be a clone: He or she would have developed from a cell derived from an embryo created with an egg and a sperm, and "improved" in the laboratory. The altered genes would be present in every cell of the child's body, and would be passed down to any and all future generations.

Many people assume that this kind of genetic manipulation—often called "inheritable genetic modification"—is necessary in order for parents who carry a gene associated with diseases such as Tay Sachs or cystic fibrosis to avoid passing it on to their children. This is not the case, and those who say it is are mistaken or intending to mislead. Using already available screening techniques, parents at risk of having children with serious genetic diseases like these can undergo in vitro fertilization and then select embryos unaffected by the condition.

Embryo selection, or "pre-implantation genetic diagnosis," is itself subject to abuse, and in need of strong regulation. Many disability rights activists argue that it is being used in a misguided search for "perfect" babies, and many feminists voice concern about its use to satisfy "gender preference." But allowing parents to select from among

> ## FAST FACT
>
> The word *eugenics* comes from the Greek word *eugenes,* which means "well-born." The eugenics movement was begun in the early twentieth century by British scientist Francis Galton. The idea was carried to its most extreme by the Nazis, who exterminated 100,000 disabled persons in the early stages of their genocidal reign.

An embryologist holds a rack of containers that are used to store frozen human embryos in liquid nitrogen as part of the in vitro fertilization process.

several embryos for serious medical reasons would have far lesser eugenic implications than would a consumer-based dynamic of "improving" future children by genetic manipulation.

This little-remarked-upon technical relationship between embryo cloning and inheritable genetic modification is a red flag. In the absence of effective regulation, it is very worrisome. And it is truly alarming in light of the ongoing efforts of noted scientists, authors, and others to make eugenic engineering seem both alluring and inevitable.

A Serious Concern

How seriously should we treat predictions of the inevitable emergence of a genetic elite and "post-human" species? We can hope that technical unreliability will block those who would like to endow future children with manipulated genes or artificial chromosomes. But transgenic animals—goats that secrete spider silk in their milk, rabbits that glow in the dark—now exist. And even if "GenRich"-type alterations remain beyond technical reach, the ideological impact of promoting them is dangerously powerful.

Marketing the ability to specify our children's appearance and abilities encourages a grotesque consumerist mentality toward children and all human life. Fostering the notion that only a "perfect baby" is worthy of life threatens our solidarity with and support for the disabled, and perpetuates unattainable standards of perfection. Channeling hopes for human betterment into preoccupation with genetic fixes shrinks our already withered commitments to improving social conditions and enriching cultural and community life. Promoting a future of genetically engineered inequality legitimizes the vast existing injustices that are socially arranged and enforced.

Critics of using genetic engineering to produce designer babies believe it would reduce childbirth to a commercial transaction.

Source: Asay. © 2001 by Creators Syndicate, Inc. Reproduced by permission.

Not a Legitimate Choice

Most advocates of eugenic engineering realize that their project all too easily triggers concerns like these, and evokes associations with Nazi racism and genocide. They counter that while the Nazis' methods were pernicious, and while governmental coercion must of course be avoided, the new eugenics would emerge out of the voluntary choices of parents-to-be who had concluded that preselecting their offspring's genes would give their children the best start in life.

This consumer's view of eugenics lends itself to the claim that designing a baby is an "individual right." But rights are always socially negotiated—not long ago, slave owning and marital rape were counted among them. And the value we properly place on individual liberty must always be balanced against our commitments to social justice and solidarity. Changing a future child's genetic makeup, and experimenting with the genetic legacy of humanity, fall outside any acceptable notion of individual rights or parental prerogatives.

The advocates of eugenic engineering are on equally shaky ground when they assert—as in titles such as *Children of Choice* and *From Chance to Choice*—that manipulating a future child's genes is a "reproductive choice." Terminating an unwanted pregnancy is very different from determining the genetic constitution of a future child.

Also suspect are claims that restrictions on inheritable genetic modification and reproductive cloning would trample scientific freedom. The capacity to manipulate the genes we pass on to our children carries social and political risks as momentous as those posed by any technology humanity has yet developed. Surely such a world-shaping technology is a proper subject for democratic control. . . .

Inheritable Genetic Modification Should Be Banned

What is to be done? Let's look at the big picture. We believe that there is widespread support, domestically and internationally, for responsible governance of the new human genetic and reproductive technologies.

First, reproductive cloning and inheritable genetic modification should be banned. These technologies serve no overriding positive purpose, and open the door to a potentially catastrophic eugenic future. . . .

Decisions about how and where to draw political and policy lines around the new human genetic and reproductive technologies are decisions about the future of humanity. They must not be left to those committed to grotesque visions of a "post-human" future, or with financial or professional stakes in particular procedures. We must ensure that the new human genetic technologies are used to advance health and well-being for all, and not hijacked in the service of a dangerous new eugenics.

EVALUATING THE AUTHOR'S ARGUMENTS:

Authors in this chapter use various phrases to describe the process of altering human DNA in ways that will be passed on to future generations. Commonly used terms include genetic enhancement, germ line engineering, and inheritable genetic modification. Marcy Darnovsky uses the phrase *eugenic engineering* to describe this process. What point do you think she is trying to make by using this term? Does it make her argument more or less persuasive? Explain.

Human Genetic Enhancement Would Be Ethical

Ted Peters

"There is no theological justification for thinking of some persons as inferior to others, and new technical possibilities in genetics ought not change this."

In the following viewpoint Ted Peters responds to arguments that are commonly made by those who oppose human genetic engineering on ethical grounds. For example, critics contend that genetic enhancement could lead to a society in which those who are enhanced are deemed superior whereas the "unenhanced" are viewed as inferior. In response to this argument, Peters contends that the concept of human dignity applies to all persons regardless of their genetic makeup. Genetic engineering will not change the inherent worth of human beings. In addition, Peters insists, there is no reason to believe that genetic engineering will lead to discrimination and prejudice against the unenhanced. Peters is a professor of systematic theology at Pacific Lutheran Theological Seminary and the Center for Theology and the Natural Sciences at the Graduate Theological Union in Berkeley, California. He is the author of *Playing God? Genetic Determinism and Human Freedom.*

AS YOU READ, CONSIDER THE FOLLOWING QUESTIONS:
1. How does Peters respond to the argument that genetic enhancement should not be pursued due to potential unexpected consequences?
2. Why do critics associate genetic engineering with Nazism, according to the author?
3. How does Peters respond to the charge that genetic engineering will lead to treating humans as artifacts?

L et us turn to a closer look at the arguments for and against germline intervention and manipulation. . . . In order to engage the issue in some detail . . . I would like to turn our attention to a representative case in point, namely, the position paper drafted by the Council for Responsible Genetics (CRG) in the fall of 1992. The CRG proffers three types of argument in opposition to germline modification in humans: a technical argument, a slanderous argument, and an ethical argument.

The first argument against germline manipulation is technical. Although the motive for modifying germ genes may be the enhancement of human well-being for future generations, unexpected deleterious consequences may result. Removal of an unwanted disease gene may not eliminate the possibility that other gene combinations will be created that will be harmful. Inadvertent damage could result from biologists' inability to predict just how genes or their products interact with one another and with the environment. "Inserting new segments of DNA into the germline could have major, unpredictable consequences for both the individual and the future of the species that include the introduction of susceptibilities to cancer and other disease into the human gene pool" [according to the CRG].

It would seem to the prudent observer that we take a "wait and see" attitude, that we move cautiously as the technology develops. . . . However, the problem of unexpected consequences is one that confronts all long-term planning, and in itself should not deter research and experimentation guided by a vision of a healthier humanity.

A Slanderous Comparison to Nazis

The second argument appeals to guilt by association and is thereby slanderous. The CRG Human Genetics Committee says "the doctrine of social advancement through biological perfectibility underlying the new eugenics is almost indistinguishable from the older version so avidly embraced by the Nazis." The structure of this argument is that because germline modification can be associated with eugenics, and because eugenics can be associated with Nazism, it follows that we can associate proponents of germline enhancement with the Nazis and, on this ground, should reject it. The argument borders on the *ad hominem* (circumstantial) fallacy.

A diabetic child fills a syringe with insulin. Advocates believe the potential of genetic engineering to cure diseases such as diabetes outweighs its possible harms.

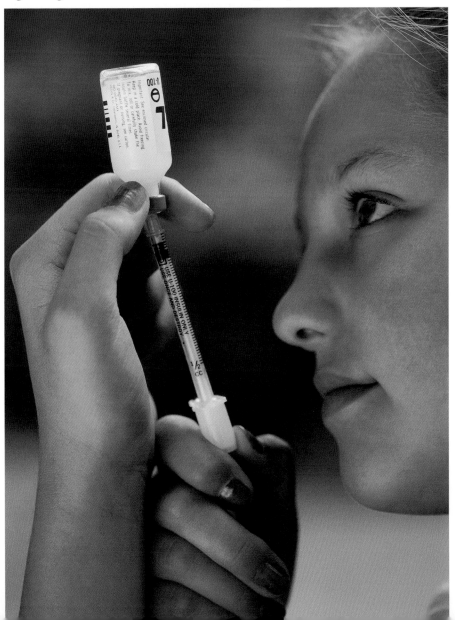

One problem is that the CRG argument is too glib, failing to discern the complexities here. The eugenics movement of the late-nineteenth and early-twentieth centuries was originally a socially progressive movement that embraced the ideals of a better society. In England and America it became tied to ethnocentrism and the blindness of class interests, leading to forced sterilization of feeble-minded prisoners. It was eventually discarded because advances in genetics proved it unscientific. In Germany the eugenics movement became tied to anti-Semitism, resulting in the racial hygiene (*Rassenhygiene*) program of the Nazi SS and the atrocities of the so-called "final solution." With this history in mind, the present generation must certain-

The research of most genetic scientists is focused on developing cures for diseases rather than creating designer babies.

ly be on guard against future programs of "ethnic hygiene" which seem to plague the human species in one form or another every century. Yet we must observe that ethnocentric bias in England and America and the rise of Nazism in Germany were social phenomena that employed eugenics for their respective ends. Eugenics is not the source of injustice, even if it can be a weapon in the service of injustice. The CRG's use of the volatile word "Nazi" in this discussion of germline enhancement is an attempt to paint their opponents in such a repulsive color that no one will open-mindedly view the matter.

Modest Aspirations

The third CRG argument, the ethical argument, is much more worthy of serious consideration. The central thesis here is that germline modification will reinforce existing social discrimination. The position paper declares,

> The cultural impact of treating humans as biologically perfectible artifacts would be entirely negative. People who fall short of some technically achievable ideal would increasingly be seen as "damaged goods." And it is clear that the standards for what is genetically desirable will be those of the society's economically and politically dominant groups. This will only reinforce prejudices and discrimination in a society where they already exist.

Let us look at this argument in terms of its component parts. The assumption in the first sentence is that germline intervention implies biological perfectibility and, on account of this, that human persons will be treated as artifacts. It is of course plausible that a social construction of the perfect child or the perfected human strain might appear in Saturday morning cartoons and other cultural forms. Yet, this does not seem to apply to the actual situation in which genetic scientists currently find themselves. They are occupied with much more modest aspirations such as protection from monogenetic diseases such as Cystic Fibrosis. The medical technology here is not much beyond infancy. At this point in technological history we do not find ourselves on the brink of designer children or the advent of a super strain. What is "genetically desirable" is by no means scientifically attainable. Thus, [biologist] Hessel Bouma and his colleagues are less worried than the

CRG because they recognize that the technological possibility of creating a genetically perfect human race is still very remote. "Things like intelligence and strength are not inherited through single genes but through multifactoral conditions, combinations of inherited genes and numerous environmental factors. Our ability to control and to design is limited by the complexity of many traits, so there are seemingly insurmountable technological and economic barriers that weaken the empirical slippery-slope argument that we are sliding into the genetic engineering of our children" [says Bouma].

Human Dignity

Continuing our analysis of the ethical argument, the CRG rightly alerts us to the social-psychology of feeling like "damaged goods" and being treated like "damaged goods." If a "technically achievable ideal" should become a cultural norm, then those who fail to meet the norm would understandably feel inferior. Furthermore, the economically and politically advantaged groups will help to steer the definition of the ideal norm to serve their own class interests. Here the CRG should be applauded for alerting us to a possible loss of human dignity.

At this point a reaffirmation of human dignity is called for, I believe, wherein each individual person is treated as having the full complement of rights regardless of his or her genes. Ethical support here comes from the Christian doctrine of creation, wherein God makes men and women in the divine image and pronounces them "good" (Genesis 1:26–31). It also comes from the ministry of Jesus, wherein the Son of God sought out the outcasts, the lame, the infirm, the possessed—surely those who were considered the "damaged goods" of first-century Palestine—for divine favor and healing. Each human being, regardless of health or social location or genetic endowment is loved by God, and this recognition should translate into social equality and mutual appreciation. There is no theological justification for thinking of some persons as inferior to others, and new technical possibilities in genetics ought not change this.

Not a Cause of Discrimination

We also note the CRG's prognostication for the future: germline modification "will only reinforce prejudices and discrimination in a soci-

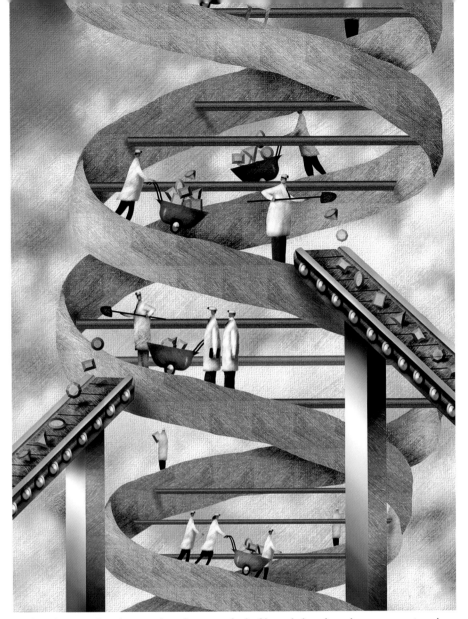

Although researchers have gathered a great deal of knowledge about human genetics, the science of human genetic manipulation is in its earliest stages.

ety where they already exist." Prejudices and discrimination exist in the present, says the CRG. This is an obvious fact we readily concede. Does it follow, however, that germline intervention "will only reinforce" them? Is germline modification the cause of present prejudice and discrimination? No. Prejudice and discrimination seem to flourish quite well without germline manipulation, yet somehow this is alleged to count as an argument against the latter.

The ABC's of Human Genetic Engineering

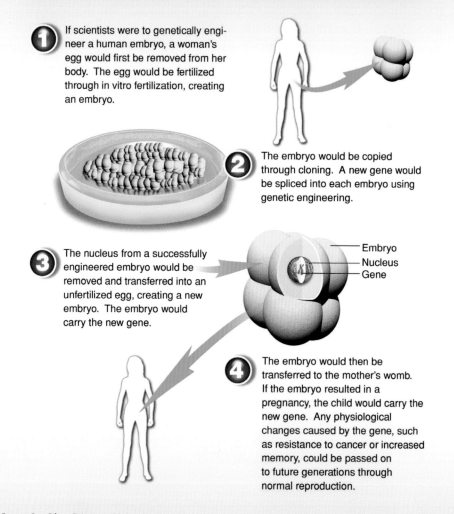

1 If scientists were to genetically engineer a human embryo, a woman's egg would first be removed from her body. The egg would be fertilized through in vitro fertilization, creating an embryo.

2 The embryo would be copied through cloning. A new gene would be spliced into each embryo using genetic engineering.

3 The nucleus from a successfully engineered embryo would be removed and transferred into an unfertilized egg, creating a new embryo. The embryo would carry the new gene.

Embryo
Nucleus
Gene

4 The embryo would then be transferred to the mother's womb. If the embryo resulted in a pregnancy, the child would carry the new gene. Any physiological changes caused by the gene, such as resistance to cancer or increased memory, could be passed on to future generations through normal reproduction.

Source: Lee Silver, Princeton University.

If the argument rests on the premise that germline enhancement will create a technical ideal achievable by some but not others, then it fails on the grounds of triviality. This could apply to countless ideals in our society. We daily confront innumerable ideals that are met by some but not all, whether they be athletic achievements, beauty trophies, professional promotions, or lottery winnings. These may elicit temporary feelings of inferiority on the part of those who come in second or further behind, but they are widely ignored by those who did not compete. Given the realistic prospects for what germline enhancement is aimed at accomplishing, the new situation would not alter the present situation in this respect. If it is technically possible to relieve some individuals from suffering the consequences of diabetes through the regular use of insulin, then the achievement of this ideal for those afflicted by diabetes leads to only gratitude on their part and on the part of those who love them. Somatic cell therapy or even germline modification for diabetes will only extend this gratitude. To those who are not afflicted or likely to be afflicted by diabetes, this achievement may be applauded from a distance or perhaps ignored.

One could envision a next step, of course, where germline intervention could, if made universally available, eliminate the likes of diabetes from the human gene pool. We would then have a future wiped clean of genetically based diabetes. If this constituted an achieved ideal for the whole human race, and if the unexpected consequences were less harmful than the diabetes, then many persons will have been spared the suffering diabetes *could* have caused and no reinforcement of prejudice and discrimination will have occurred.

What if we were to falter somewhere along the way? Suppose we began a worldwide program to eliminate the predisposition to diabetes from the human gene pool, achieved success in some family or ethnic or class groups, and then due to lack of funding or other factors had to abandon the project. What would happen to those individuals who still carried the deleterious gene? Would they suffer stigma or discrimination? Perhaps, yes. And the CRG rightly alerts us to such a possibility. Yet, we might ask, does this prospect provide sufficient warrant to shut down the research and prohibit embarking on such a plan?

EVALUATING THE AUTHOR'S ARGUMENTS:

Analyze Peters's responses to each of the three arguments against genetic enhancement. Are his arguments persuasive? Defend your answers using references to this viewpoint and/or other viewpoints in this chapter.

Genetic Enhancement Will Improve Humanity

George Dvorsky

"A . . . movement has . . . emerged that is committed to the goal of human enhancement with the eventual goal of seeing humanity emerge into a posthuman species."

In the following viewpoint George Dvorsky argues that genetic engineering could elevate the human race to a new level. Dvorsky is dismayed that even many genetic scientists oppose using the technology for human enhancement. He attributes this lack of support to various cultural influences, including conservative bioethicists who are in charge of shaping the policies that guide U.S. medical research. However, Dvorsky contends that a growing group of scientists, ethicists, and philosophers advocate using genetic enhancement to make humans better. George Dvorsky is the deputy editor of Betterhumans, an editorial production company whose goal is to advance science and technology. He is also the president of the Toronto Transhumanist Association, a nonprofit organization that promotes the use of technology to improve human health and potential.

1. How do the media contribute to the public's opposition to human genetic engineering, according to Dvorsky?
2. How does the author respond to the argument that practical obstacles make human genetic engineering impossible?
3. What is James Watson's position on genetic enhancement, as quoted by the author?

I n 1997, Gregory Stock, author of *Redesigning Humans: Our Inevitable Genetic Future,* approached the Biotech Industry Organization [BIO] for funding to support a symposium on engineering the human germline—making human genetic modifications that will get passed to future generations.

It was to be the first large public discussion of this controversial but important topic. But surprisingly, BIO turned Stock down. As he notes, "Not only did they say no, they urged me not to hold the event and told me that what I was attempting was highly irresponsible because it might create a backlash against important biotechnology."

My own experiences mirror this story. I've spoken to prospective cognitive scientists and biotechnologists whose jaws have dropped when I dared suggest that the results of their labour be applied to bettering the human physical condition. As one student of artificial intelligence said to me, "It is as if you believe that as a society we actually know what's good for us in the long run, which, from the state of the environment, homelessness, crime, psychological illness, and impending war these days, seems a rather hard position to defend."

What's going on here? The momentum created by Enlightenment positivism was all but quashed during the 20th century, and resultant

> ## FAST FACT
>
> A *Luddite* is a person who opposes technological change. The word comes from the name of a mythical figure known as Ned Ludd, or King Ludd. The original Luddites were a group of English textile workers in the early nineteenth century who began destroying knitting machines, which the Luddites blamed for putting people out of work.

Approval of Using Genetic Technology

Men
Women

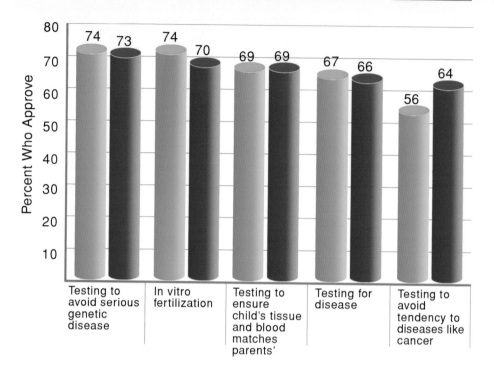

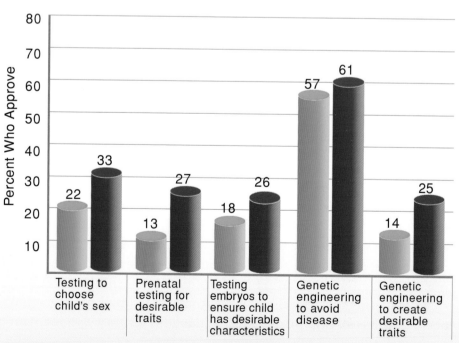

Source: "Public Awareness and Attitudes About Genetic Technology," survey prepared by Princeton Survey Research Associates for the Genetics and Public Policy Center, October 2002.

social taboos about meddling with the human organism have crept into laboratories and academic hallways. Most of the scientists who are making it possible balk completely at the prospect of redesigning humans, while promoting neo-Luddism [opposition to technology]. When in history have scientists been described as Luddites?

Fifty years after the discovery of DNA's structure, however, things look set to change. Conscious human redesign may not be acceptable dinner conversation today, but it is definitely gaining support amongst scientists, philosophers and bioethicists.

Reasons for Opposition

There are a number of reasons why scientists have been opposed to using their genetic knowledge to improve the human organism, most of them culturally rooted.

Religions, media, the entertainment industry and some conservative and reactionary "bioethicists" have promoted a negative image of

James Watson (second from right) and his colleagues announce their successful mapping of the human genome at a February 2001 press conference.

human-focused biotechnology. And the public, for the most part, has bought into it.

Much of this stems from the unfortunate linkage between Nazi eugenics and any human genetic improvement. Many observers quite incorrectly equate the state-enforced sterilization practices of the Nazis with such things as assistive reproductive technologies that help parents have healthier children. Similarly, many consider the creation of a "superman" to be dangerously hubristic and reckless. . . .

And, of course, very few positive messages about genetically engineering humans ever get out to the public. The media often calls upon bioethicists who provide the cautionary message for every story. As [American bioethicist James] Hughes notes, "The media's job is to find an ethicist who has a problem with each new innovation so they have something to report."

Practical and Moral Objections

To be fair, many of the scientists that oppose human reengineering cite logistical and technological hurdles. Some credible biotechnologists perceive the quest for human redesign as an unrealistic pipedream, a process so mired in complexity that we should never attempt it.

Nelson Wivel, who served on the National Institutes of Health's Recombinant DNA Advisory Committee, is one of these scientists. "The risks of [gene therapy] will never be eliminated, and mistakes would be irreversible," he says. "Germline gene modification will always be associated with the risk of unpredictable genetic side effects, and for this reason it never should be approved for human use."

Well, never is a mighty long time. As Stock argues, to conclude that we cannot surmount the technical and scientific obstacles is premature to say the least. So while the practical objections have value, they are somewhat overblown.

Of course, not all scientists fall back on this line of thinking. Some, most notably French Anderson, the physician who performed the first human gene therapy, adamantly oppose germline enhancement on moral grounds. Anderson maintains that "the only protection for our society to prevent us tumbling down a slippery slope to a *Gattaca*-style[1] society is to insert clear stopping points along the route."

1. *Gattaca* is a 1997 science fiction film that depicts a society divided into two classes: the genetically engineered, who are considered superior, and the nongenetically engineered, who are deemed inferior.

Genetic researchers like these seek to discover the genetic causes of common diseases. Other researchers, however, wish to go beyond studying diseases and transform the human species.

Anderson insists that gene therapy should be used for no other purpose than the treatment of serious disease, no matter how tempting it might be to try to improve humans with the technology.

James Watson: Go for Perfection

Anderson and others like him, however, face a growing movement in favour of redesigning humans, a movement with one very important man as an unofficial spokesperson.

In October of last year [2002], James Watson, who along with Francis Crick discovered the structure of DNA in 1953, addressed a packed house of biology students at the University of Toronto's MacLeod Auditorium. The topic—one near-and-dear to Watson—was the

genetic engineering of humans. "Going for perfection was something I always thought you should do," proclaimed Watson, both stunning and delighting the students. "It's my impression that none of the genome-project leaders have gotten up and said, 'What we are going to do with this information; I think we should use it,'" he told the audience.

Watson, the granddaddy of genetics, fears that society will be too scared to use genetic engineering to make people as good as they can be. And he notes that far too many of his colleagues don't dare discuss such efforts. "The biggest ethical problem we have," says Watson, "is not using our knowledge."

At the tender age of 74, Watson presses his case relentlessly. He promotes a vision of the future in which couples can screen embryos for genetic diseases and participate in

Marvin Minsky, a professor at the Massachusetts Institute of Technology, is among those who advocate using genetic engineering to improve human beings.

the germline engineering of their offspring so that beneficial genetic alterations can get passed on to future generations.

Changing Minds

Watson is joined by a number of prominent bioethicists, including Hughes, John Fletcher, Peter Singer and Jonathan Glover, who have been defending the legitimacy of human enhancement. They support germinal choice, reproductive freedoms and a non-anthropocentric personhood theory of value. "As the issues become more practical, biopolitics are moving from bioethicist's academic debates to hardening battle lines," says Hughes. "We are charting a new course for bioethics."

A number of scientists are also emerging to challenge the status quo. People such as Stock, Greg Pence, Carl Djerassi, Marvin Minsky, Hans

Moravec, Ray Kurzweil, Rodney Brooks and Kevin Warwick promote important ideas about where humanity can take itself, and what challenges we might face in the future.

A coalescing and burgeoning movement has also emerged that is committed to the goal of human enhancement with the eventual goal of seeing humanity emerge into a posthuman species: The Transhumanists. This group, which claims philosophers Nick Bostrom and Max More among its ranks, welcomes the development of such things as genetic modifications.

And why not? As long as we remain diligent and insist on maintaining reproductive autonomy for prospective parents, fears of a totalitarian-like eugenics regime will remain in the realm of paranoid fantasies and bad science fiction movies.

The times are truly changing. No longer is debate about redesigning humans one-sided. There's a bioethics battle brewing between those in favour and those against. The question now is this: Which side will those doing the research choose?

EVALUATING THE AUTHOR'S ARGUMENTS:

George Dvorsky describes opponents of genetic enhancement as *Luddites*. This term is typically used to deride people who resist technological change and imply that they are hopelessly backward in their thinking. Does Dvorsky's use of this label make his argument more or less persuasive? Please explain your answer. As you read the next viewpoint, consider whether Dvorsky would characterize the author, Bill McKibben, as a Luddite. Do you think this is a fair charge? Why or why not?

Humanity Can Improve Without Genetic Enhancement

Bill McKibben

"We're close enough to the good life that we don't require a magical genetic rescue."

In the following viewpoint Bill McKibben responds to the arguments of those who advocate using genetic technology to help human beings develop to a stage beyond Homo sapiens. McKibben insists that there is no need to use technology to improve the human race because human beings are acceptable as they are. Furthermore, he argues, humanity has improved without the aid of genetic engineering and will continue to do so in the future. Bill McKibben is a scholar in residence at Middlebury College in Vermont and the author of *Enough: Staying Human in an Engineered Age*.

AS YOU READ, CONSIDER THE FOLLOWING QUESTIONS:
1. According to Robert Ettinger, as quoted by the author, what is wrong with the human mouth?
2. How does Marvin Minsky, as quoted by McKibben, characterize human beings?
3. What evidence does McKibben give to support his view that humanity has improved?

We need to do an unlikely thing: we need to survey the world we now inhabit and proclaim it good. Good enough. Not in every detail; there are a thousand improvements, technological and cultural, that we can and should still make. But good enough in its outlines, in its essentials. We need to decide that we live, most of us in the West, long enough. We need to declare that, in the West, where few of us work ourselves to the bone, we have ease enough. . . . We need to declare that we have enough stuff. Enough intelligence. Enough capability. Enough.

That's the hinge on which this argument turns. I have no shiny new vision to compete with the futurists who dream of making us "posthuman." We need, instead, a new way of looking at the present. If we can come to see it as sufficient for our needs, then perhaps we can figure out how to avoid these new technologies and the risks—physical and existential—that they pose. Perhaps we can find, instead, some conserving instinct within us that lets us stand pat [firm]. We'll get to the specifics of how we might do such a thing later, for clearly it will be difficult to blunt our technological momentum. But first we need to answer the novel question of whether we really do pass muster in our present form.

Self-Loathing Futurists

The technological visionaries shout *No!* to that question; in their eyes, we are deeply flawed, beginning with our very bodies. Consider Robert Ettinger, the world's most influential cryogenicist,[1] who said early and often that genetic engineering and other new technologies would usher in a "golden age." One prominent feature of which would be, in his opinion, the "elimination of elimination."

> ### FAST FACT
>
> In 2001, scientists completed mapping the human genome. They had expected humans to contain 100,000 genes. Instead, they found that a human being has only 30,000 to 40,000 genes. This discovery has led experts to believe that each gene has more than one function; therefore, removing or inserting a gene can have unpredictable consequences.

---

1. Cryogenicists believe that terminally ill people can be frozen until science discovers a cure for their disease, at which time they can be reanimated and cured.

If, he reasoned, "cleanliness is next to godliness, then a superman must be cleaner than a man. In the future, our plumbing (of the thawed as well as the newborn) will be more hygienic and seemly. Those who choose to will consume only zero-residue foods, with excess water all evaporating via the pores. Alternatively, modified organs may occasionally expel small, dry compact residues." Ettinger had trouble with other orifices as well: one of his friends had pointed out to him that a "multi-purpose mouth" was "awkward and primitive" to the point of "absurdity. An alien would find it most remarkable that we had an organ combining the requirements of breathing, ingesting, tasting, chewing, biting, and on occasion fighting, helping to thread needles, yelling, whistling, lecturing, and grimacing."

Ettinger was not alone in his self-loathing. It permeates this subculture, the constant lament that at best people resemble, say, Yugos—decent basic technology at a reasonable price, but nothing to get fixated on. To a technician's eye, their defects are simply too annoying. [Austrian robotics expert] Hans Moravec once reflected on . . . [a science fiction writer Isaac] Asimov short story about an android who wanted to become a real person. "That's a cute story," he said. "But I read it and I thought, *Why in hell do you want to become a man when you're something better to begin with?* It's like a human being wanting to become an *ape*. 'Gee, I really wish I had more hair, that I stooped more, smelled worse, lived a shorter life span.'"

Dispairing Visionaries

Some people, admits the AI [artificial intelligence] pioneer Marvin Minsky, seem to "like themselves just as they are. Perhaps they are not selfish enough, or imaginative, or ambitious. Myself, I don't much like how people are now. We're too shallow, slow, and ignorant." As a species, he notes, we "seem to have reached a plateau in our intellectual development. There's no sign that we're getting smarter . . . has any playwright in recent years topped [William] Shakespeare or Euripides? We have learned a lot in two thousand years, yet much ancient wisdom still seems sound, which makes me suspect that we haven't been making much progress." Basically, he maintains, it's a hardware problem: citing a Bell Labs study, he calculates that humans

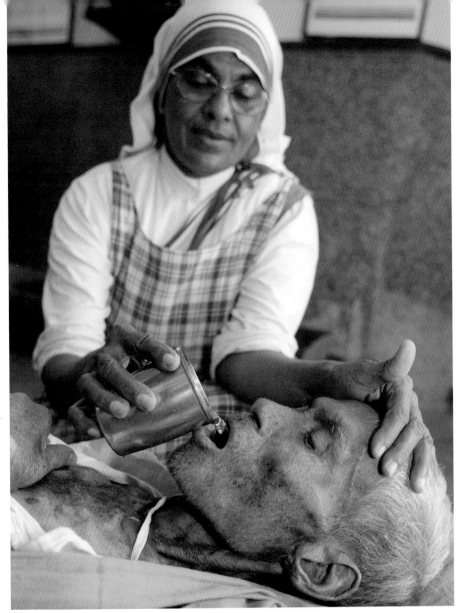

Despite their flaws, human beings are capable of altruism and compassion. Here, a nun in India feeds a terminally ill man.

can learn and remember only about two bits per second. So even if you did nothing but learn twelve hours a day for a hundred years, the total would only be about three billion bits—"less than what we can store today on a regular five-inch compact disk." . . .

But it's not just our bodies and minds that seem impossibly crude. When they look at the societies those bodies and minds have built, the visionaries despair as well—they sound, in fact, like over the top

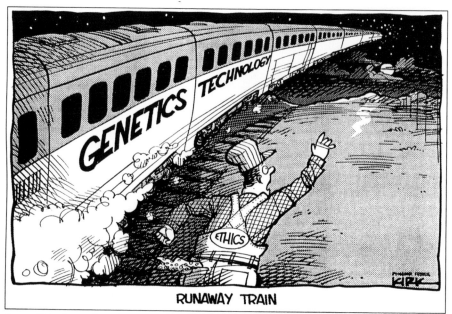

RUNAWAY TRAIN

Source: Kirk. © 1998 by Kirk Anderson. Reproduced by permission.

Hobbesians.[2] George Gilder, usually described as a "high priest" of Silicon Valley for his influential articles and seminars, says only wave after wave of high-tech change can save "millions or even billions of people from their immemorial fate as members of a barbarian mob, plunged in ignorance." On the bulletin boards of the Web, you can find zealous "transhumanists" not just explaining how the world will evolve past our species, but also debating questions like whether it's morally necessary to kill "Luddites" [people who oppose technological change] who stand in the way of such progress: "If we don't establish a transhuman future, then Planet Earth is doomed to a rather dismal malthusian[3] extermination from disease, hunger, and lack of resources. If we don't build a transhuman future, billions of people WILL die. . . . What do you intend to do about it? To what ends are you willing to save billions of lives? What means are you willing to accept to achieve those ends?" [A quote from Exropian Web digest.] . . .

That mood leaves one vulnerable to the siren song of posthumanism—to the idea that we should be radically reconfigured or, better yet, sur-

2. a reference to English philosopher Thomas Hobbes, who described human existence as bleak and cruel
3. a reference to English economist Thomas Malthus, who predicted that human population growth would inevitably lead to massive deaths from war, famine, and plague

passed by some wiser race. To the idea that new technology will save us from ourselves. . . .

Humanity Is Good
But there's another possibility. We could drop the misanthropy and look at ourselves with clearer eyes. Yes, we've damaged the environment, we've enslaved our fellow man, we've slaughtered on a vast scale.

Some people argue that sophisticated genetic technology will not necessarily improve the human condition.

"Scientists have isolated the gene that makes scientists want to isolate genes."

Source: Glasbergen. © 1999 by Rand Glasbergen. Reproduced by Permission.

This is the truth. But it's not the whole truth, or even the main one. To put it bluntly, *the fight to ward off a posthuman future begins with at least a muted celebration of the human present.*

People are okay. I'm okay, you're okay, the lady who stands there forever talking with the cashier at Shop 'n Save is nonetheless, deep down, okay. Maybe even more than okay—as birds have been blessed with flight, we have been blessed with an exuberant consciousness that has given rise to much good. So much more good than bad. The God of Genesis looks around the newborn creation and pronounces it *all* good. Not just the sun and the stars, not just the plants yielding seed and the trees bearing fruit, not just the "great sea monsters" and "everything that creeps upon the ground." Us, too. Even though we've done enormous damage. Even though we use the same mouth to eat and kiss.

And there's more. We're capable of getting better still, all on our own. We're capable of the further transformations necessary to redeem the world. Humanity is not, in the words of . . . [Gregory S. Paul and Earl Cox], "running out of steam . . . by deep-set flaws that will always limit our minds' potential." We've made a hash of the world in many ways, but the damage is not beyond repair. We're close enough to the good life that we don't require a magical genetic rescue. . . .

Slowly, but with reasonable steadiness, we've made the world less . . . Hobbesian. Legalized slavery has been scrubbed from most of its corners; we now indict as international war criminals those who rule by the normal methods of an earlier day. Most of the Western world has dispensed with capital punishment, and even in the United States we seem to weary a bit of its use. In the lifetimes of people not yet old we have seen the end to official racism, and the galloping emancipation of women in cultures across the globe. The "handicapped" are brought more fully into the life of our society; difference of every kind,

Life has improved for many women around the world, such as these schoolgirls in Afghanistan, without the use of genetic technology.

in fact, is more accepted and celebrated. It's been a bloody century we've endured; in the wake of World War II, the philosopher Robert Nozick made what he called "the argument from Hitler"—that the Holocaust demonstrated it would be no "special tragedy" were man to disappear. But you could as easily make the argument from Eisenhower: that millions were willing to fight against that tyranny, just as people fought to upend the bleak Communist totalitarianisms.

EVALUATING THE AUTHORS' ARGUMENTS:

George Dvorsky and Bill McKibben present fundamentally opposing views regarding the desirability of improving the human species by means of technology. After reading both viewpoints, do you believe the human race is "good enough," as McKibben says, or in need of improvement, as Dvorsky claims? Please explain your answer using examples from the viewpoints.

CHAPTER 2

Is the Genetic Engineering of Plants and Animals Beneficial?

Protesters demonstrate their concerns about the safety of foods produced with genetic technology.

Genetically Engineered Crops Threaten Human Health and the Environment

Sierra Club

"Plants are complex and introducing new genes may result in unanticipated changes."

The Sierra Club is an organization that works to protect the enviroment. In the following viewpoint, written in a question-and-answer format, the club argues that genetically engineered crops pose several threats to human health and the environment. Little is known about the long-term effects of transferring alien genes into plants, according to the Sierra Club. Therefore, people consuming food derived from genetically modified crops could be at an increased risk for toxic poisoning, allergic reactions, and antibiotic resistance. In addition, the authors contend, these crops pose significant risks to the environment. Crops that have been genetically engineered to resist herbicides could spread and crossbreed with surrounding crops or wild plants. This gene transfer could result in the emergence of new weeds that are hard to kill and that could damage other crops or valuable native species. In addition, plants that are bioengineered to contain their own pesticides might poison the soil and kill beneficial insects.

AS YOU READ, CONSIDER THE FOLLOWING QUESTIONS:
1. What types of genes are being spliced into foods, according to the Sierra Club?
2. What are the risks posed by crops engineered with the Bt toxin, as stated by the authors?
3. What is "Terminator" technology, as defined by the Sierra Club?

There is international consumer backlash against a new form of pollution: genes from viruses, bacteria and animals being spliced into food crops. While the U.S. is promoting genetically engineered foods, many nations throughout the world have been enacting laws and policies that restrict the use of genetically engineered products in their foods.

What is genetic engineering? Genetic engineering is a radical technology involving the manipulation of genes. Scientists can transfer genes from one species to another totally unrelated species. For example, genes from an animal can be transferred to a plant, to make a new life form. This technology allows scientists to bypass the natural barriers which protect the genetic integrity of species. Genetic engineering goes far beyond conventional breeding and hybridization.

What is being gene-spliced into foods? Genes from bacteria (including those for antibiotic resistance), viruses, insects, nuts, fish, and animals are presently spliced into common food crops or are on the way. Presently, ⅔ of processed foods are made with a genetically engineered organism (GEO).

> **FAST FACT**
>
> According to the Council for Responsible Genetics, researchers in Australia have discovered that a canola plant can cross-pollinate with a plant from a related species located as far as three kilometers away.

Effects on Human Health

How will my health be affected by genetically engineered food? There is no requirement for long term testing and therefore, much is unknown. Plants are complex and introducing new genes may result in unanticipated changes. New toxins and allergens, changes in nutritional benefits, and spread of antibiotic resistance may occur.

How can I choose to avoid eating genetically engineered foods (GEFs)? No laws exist to label genetically engineered foods, so there is no right-to-know or freedom of choice. No foods grown organically have been genetically engineered. Purchasing organic food is an excellent way to avoid consuming GEFs.

Effects on the Environment

What are the ecological consequences? Species have been evolving over millions of years. The ecological impact from the spread of genetic contamination is largely unknown. Pollen can be carried by wind and bees over a range of distances. Farm to farm spread of transgenes (genetically engineered genes) can be widespread. Transgenes can spread to wild relatives and these genes can become established in nature.

Many Americans are unaware that about two-thirds of the processed foods they consume contain genetically engineered ingredients.

Crops that are engineered to resist infestation from insects may pose risks to nonpests such as the Monarch butterfly.

Genes conferring resistance to weedkillers are becoming "promiscuous" and spreading to surrounding weeds, making those weeds invulnerable to some herbicides. Pest resistance can also spread into nature. The resulting plants might have the ability to outcompete native species in the environment and destroy natural biological systems.

Many crops are engineered with the Bt toxin, in order to resist infestation from insects. Yet root exudates [exuded matter] from these plants release the toxin into the soil, where it retains its activity long after its release. This stimulates major changes in soil . . . that could affect nutrient cycling processes and reduce soil fertility.

The Bt toxin is also lethal to nontarget organisms, such as Monarch butterflies, lacewings and ladybird [ladybug] beetles. Lacewings and ladybug beetles play an important role in maintaining the equilibrium of insect populations. But the issue is broader than whether Bt toxin produced by genetically modified crops imperils Monarch butterflies. The

real issue is that a strategy to establish expression of an insecticidal compound in large-scale crop monocultures [large farms that grow a single crop] and thus expose a homogeneous subecosystem continuously to the toxin can cause irreparable damage to natural habitats, forever.

How might organic farming be affected? The entire future of organic farming could be threatened. Pollen can transfer genetically engineered genes into previously organic crops. It is also expected that Bt, the natural insecticide used in organic farming, will lose its effectiveness.

What is the "Terminator" technology? This technology makes crops sterile. It's a global threat to the food supply and violates farmers' rights to save seeds. The U.S. Department of Agriculture shares the patent, so our taxpaying dollars are supporting this!

Feeding the World

Are genetically engineered foods needed to feed the world? No. Hunger does not have to do with lack of food or the capacity to grow it. People go hungry when they don't have land on which to grow food or the money to buy it.

African delegates to the United Nations, in 1998, stated, "We . . . strongly object that the image of the poor and hungry from our countries is being used by giant multinational corporations to push a technology that is neither safe, environmentally friendly, nor economically beneficial to us. We do not believe that such companies or gene technologies will help our farmers to produce the food that is needed in the 21st century. On the contrary, we think it will destroy the diversity, the local knowledge and the sustainable agricultural systems that our farmers have developed for millennia and that it will thus undermine our capacity to feed ourselves."

Are there further concerns about genetic engineering and nature? GEOs are patented (owned and controlled) by huge corporations. We believe that the genetic code, which has evolved over billions of years, should remain the shared, common heritage of us all. As trees and other plant life, fish and other animals, and insects and microbes are genetically engineered for short-term profit, the fundamental blueprints of the natural world are changed forever. More attention needs to be given to ethical and societal values and the rights of indigenous people. Public input is urgently needed.

EVALUATING THE AUTHORS' ARGUMENTS:

In the viewpoint you just read, the Sierra Club argues that the genetic engineering of plants is fundamentally different from conventional breeding practices. How is it different, in their opinion? In the next viewpoint, Channapatna S. Prakash and Gregory Conko contend that genetic engineering is essentially the same as traditional plant breeding. Which viewpoint is more convincing on this point, and why? Why is this issue important in the debate over the risks of genetically engineered crops?

Genetically Engineered Crops Do Not Threaten Human Health and the Environment

Channapatna S. Prakash and Gregory Conko

"Genetically modified crops will pose no new or heightened risks that can not be identified and mitigated."

In the following viewpoint Channapatna S. Prakash and Gregory Conko reject the charge that genetically engineered crops threaten human health and the environment. They insist that genetic modification is nothing new in agriculture and that plant breeders have been changing the genetic makeup of crops for centuries. Genetic engineering of plants, also known as gene splicing or recombinant DNA technology, is simply a more precise version of traditional plant breeding. Prakash and Conko also contend that foods derived from genetically modified plants may even be safer than those produced using traditional farming methods due to the precision of the technology and the testing that GE foods are subjected to.

In addition, they maintain, little risk exists of genetically modified plants crossbreeding with wild plants and harming the environment. Instead, they contend that agricultural biotechnology will benefit the environment by requiring less acreage for farmland and fewer chemical herbicides and pesticides. Channapatna S. Prakash is a professor of plant biotechnology at Tuskegee University in Alabama. Gregory Conko is a senior fellow and the director of food safety policy at the Competitive Enterprise Institute, a public interest group based in Washington, D.C.

AS YOU READ, CONSIDER THE FOLLOWING QUESTIONS:

1. In how many countries are genetically engineered crops grown, as reported by the authors?
2. Why will the environmental risks of genetic engineering of crops be minimal and manageable, according to Prakash and Conko?
3. What risk do the authors say is greater than the threat of a genetically modified plant "running amok"?

All modern crops are a product of various genetic meddling. Recombinant DNA methods can therefore be seen as an extension of the continuum of techniques used to modify organisms over the millennia. The biggest difference is that modern genetically modified crops involve a precise transfer of one or two known genes into plant DNA—a surgical alteration of the crop's genome compared to the sledgehammer approaches of traditional hybridization or mutagenesis. Furthermore, unlike varieties developed from more conventional breeding, modern genetically modified crops are rigorously tested and subject to intense regulatory scrutiny prior to commercialization.

There has been widespread acceptance and support for recombinant DNA modification from the scientific community, plant breeders and farmers. Accumulated experience and knowledge of decades of crop improvement combined with expert judgment, science-based reasoning and empirical research has generated confidence that modern genetically modified crops will pose no new or heightened risks

Researchers have altered the DNA of plants to give them traits such as increased resistance to cold weather, diseases, and parasites.

that can not be identified and mitigated, and that any unforeseen hazards are likely to be negligible and manageable.

Many growers have embraced modern genetically modified technology because it makes farming more efficient, protects or increases yields and reduces their reliance on chemicals that, other things being equal, they would prefer not to use. Crops enhanced with recombinant DNA technology are now [as of 2003] grown on nearly 58 million hectares in 16 countries. More importantly, more than three-quarters of the 5.5 million growers who benefit from genetically modified crops are resource-poor farmers in the developing world.

Unfounded Safety Concerns

Ingredients produced from modern genetic modification are found in thousands of food products consumed worldwide. Yet, even though no legitimate evidence of harm to human health or the environment from these foods is known or expected, there is an intense debate questioning the value and safety of genetically modified organisms.

Although it may seem reasonable for consumers to express a concern that they "don't know what they're eating with genetically modified foods," . . . consumers never had that information with conventionally modified crops either. Indeed, while no assurance of perfect safety can be made, breeders know far more about the genetic make-up, product characteristics and safety of every modern genetically modified crop than those of any conventional variety ever marketed. Breeders know exactly what new genetic material has been introduced. They can identify where the transferred genes have been inserted into the new plant. They can test to ensure that transferred genes are working properly and that the nutritional elements of the food have been unchanged. None of these safety assurances can be made with conventional breeding techniques.

Consider, for example, how conventional plant breeders would develop a disease-resistant tomato. Sexual reproduction introduces chromosome fragments from a wild relative to transfer a gene for disease resistance into cultivated varieties. In the process, hundreds of unknown and unwanted genes are also introduced, with the risk that some of them could encode toxins or allergens. Yet regulators never

Scientists hope that studying the genetics of plants will improve techniques for raising crops.

routinely test conventionally bred plant varieties for food safety or environmental risk factors, and they are subject to practically no government oversight.

We have always lived with food risks. But modern genetic technology makes it increasingly easier to reduce those risks.

What About the Environment?

Do modern genetically modified crops really pose even greater environmental risks [than traditional farming methods], as critics claim?

The risk of cross-pollination from crops to wild relatives has always existed, and such "gene flow" occurs whenever crops grow in close proximity to sexually compatible wild relatives. Yet breeders have continuously introduced genes for disease and pest resistance through conventional breeding into all of our crops. Traits, such as stress tolerance and herbicide resistance, have also been introduced in some

Today, many farmers use genetically modified crops as a way to increase crop yields and cut costs.

crops with conventional techniques, and the growth habits of every crop have been altered. Thus, not only is gene modification a common phenomenon, but so are many of the specific kinds of changes made with recombinant DNA techniques.

Risks Will Be Minimal

Naturally, with both conventional and recombinant DNA-enhanced breeding, we must be vigilant to ensure that newly introduced plants do not become invasive and that weeds do not become noxious as a result of genetic modification. Although modern genetic modification expands the range of new traits that can be added to crop plants, it also ensures that more will be known about those traits and that the behavior of the modified plants will be, in many ways, easier to predict. That greater knowledge, combined with historical experience with conventional genetic modification, provides considerable assurance that such risks will be minimal and manageable.

It should also be comforting to recognize that no major weed or invasiveness problems have developed since the advent of modern plant breeding, because domesticated plants are typically poorly fit for survival in the wild. Indeed, concerns about genetically modified crops running amok, or errant genes flowing into wild species—sometimes characterized as "gene pollution"—pale in comparison to the genuine risk posed by introducing totally unmodified "exotic" plants into new ecosystems. Notable examples of the latter include

FAST FACT

Many different terms are used to refer to genetic engineering for agricultural purposes. Commonly used expressions include gene splicing, recombinant DNA technology, and agricultural biotechnology. Plants and animals produced using this technology are known as genetically modified organisms (GMOs). Foods derived from genetically engineered crops are known as genetically engineered foods, GE foods, genetically modified foods, or GM foods. They are sometimes derisively referred to as "Frankenfoods," a reference to the horror novel *Frankenstein,* in which a mad scientist creates a live man from the body parts of dead people.

Source: Benson. © 1999 by the *Arizona Republic*. Reproduced by permission of United Feature Syndicate, Inc.

water hyacinth in Lake Victoria, cord-grass in China, cattail in Nigeria and kudzu in North America.

This is, of course, not to say that no harm could ever come from the introduction of modern genetically modified or conventionally modified crop varieties. Some traits, if transferred from crops to wild relatives, could increase the reproductive fitness of weeds and cause them to become invasive or to erode the genetic diversity of native flora. But the magnitude of that risk has solely to do with the traits involved, the plants into which they are transferred and the environment into which they are introduced. Consequently, breeders, farmers and regulators are aware of the possibility that certain traits introduced into any new crop varieties, or new varieties introduced into different ecosystems, could pose genuine problems, and these practices are carefully scrutinized. Again, though, this risk occurs regardless of the breeding method used to introduce those traits into the crop.

Environmental Benefits of Genetically Modified Crops

Finally, one must also recognize the potential positive impact of recombinant DNA modified crops on the environment. Already, commercialized genetically modified crops have reduced agricultural expansion and promoted ecosystem preservation, improved air, soil and water quality as a consequence of reduced tillage, chemical spraying and fuel use and enhanced biodiversity because of lower insecticide use.

Studies have shown that the eight most common modern genetically modified crops grown in the US alone increased crop yields by nearly 2 billion kilograms, provided a net value of US$1.5 billion and reduced pesticide use by 20 million kilograms. A 2002 Council for Agricultural Science and Technology report also found that recombinant DNA modified crops promote the adoption of conservation tillage practices, resulting in many other important environmental benefits: 37 million tons of topsoil preserved, 85% reduction in greenhouse gas emissions from farm machinery, 70% reduction in herbicide runoff, 90% decrease in soil erosion and from 15 to 26 liters of fuel saved per acre.

EVALUATING THE AUTHORS' ARGUMENTS:

The viewpoint you just read differs from the previous viewpoint's assessment of the risks posed by the spread of genetically modified plants to neighboring crops and wild vegetation. Summarize the two viewpoints' arguments on this issue. Which viewpoint is more persuasive, and why?

Genetically Modified Crops Will Help Developing Nations

Florence Wambugu

> *"I am a passionate believer in the power of biotechnology to boost food production and fight hunger and poverty in the developing world."*

In October 2002 the African country Zambia refused to accept a shipment of American food aid because it consisted of genetically modified corn. Despite a severe food shortage in the country, Zambia's president, Levy Mwanawasa, described the food aid as "poison" and said he would not accept it due to the potential health and environmental risks it posed. Many leaders both inside and outside of Africa criticized this decision, arguing that the risks posed by genetically modified foods were outweighed by the impending starvation of millions of Zambians. However, the issue was complicated by trade policies. The European Union, Zambia's primary trading partner, forbade trading with countries that allowed genetically modified crops. Zambia feared that the aid corn would taint its own crops, damaging its trade relations with European countries and harming its economy.

Florence Wambugu, testimony before the U.S. House Committee on Agriculture, Washington, DC, March 26, 2003.

Zambia's refusal of genetically modified food aid focused international attention on the potential of biotechnology to help feed developing nations. The current world population exceeds 6 billion people, and that number is expected to surpass 8 billion by 2030. Some proponents of genetic engineering argue that agricultural biotechnology can help feed this growing population and prevent famines, especially in developing regions such as India and Africa. This is the position argued in the following viewpoint by Florence Wambugu. Focusing specifically on Africa, Wambugu maintains that Zambia was wrong to refuse the genetically engineered corn (although she sympathizes with the nation's predicament). Moreover, she contends that the use of genetic engineering technology can greatly increase the continent's output of corn, sweet potatoes, and bananas. While there are potential risks associated with genetically modified foods, Wambugu admits, the benefits of preventing malnutrition and starvation outweigh the harms these foods may cause.

Florence Wambugu is the founder and chief executive officer of Africa Harvest Biotech Foundation International, an organization that promotes the use of biotechnology to fight hunger, malnutrition, and poverty in Africa and the developing world.

AS YOU READ, CONSIDER THE FOLLOWING QUESTIONS:

1. On what two false premises is opposition to the use of biotechnology in Africa founded, according to the author?
2. To what commonplace—but potentially risky—technology does the author compare agricultural biotechnology?
3. Why have African farmers embraced agricultural biotechnology, as reported by Wambugu?

I am a passionate believer in the power of biotechnology to boost food production and fight hunger and poverty in the developing world. As one of nine children growing up on a small farm in Kenya, I know that African farmers need more tools for fighting plant diseases and overcoming other barriers to increased crop production. I do not believe that biotechnology is a silver bullet for African agriculture, but it is an indispensable tool that can have dramatic benefits.

The African continent, more than any other, urgently needs agricultural biotechnology, including transgenic crops, to improve food production. This is why the debate over providing genetically modified (GM) corn in food aid shipments is so troubling. The primary accomplishment of the mainly European anti-biotech lobby, through gross misinformation and political maneuvering, was only to keep safe and nutritious food out of the hands of starving people.

Africans Support Biotech Agriculture

However, these cynical organizations also used famine as an opportunity to promote an anti-biotech message that not only undermines the most promising developments in African agriculture, but also further distorts the global debate over biotechnology. African scientists, who overwhelmingly support the development of biotechnology for African agriculture, have a common interest with you in fighting for open minds and markets around the world.

It is a paradox that one of the most controversial sciences—biotechnology—has become a unifying factor for African scientists. Given the controversies surrounding the science, arriving at a consensus position has not been easy. But biotechnology has gained acceptance because there is consensus that it is a global opportunity. Both multi-

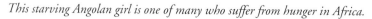

This starving Angolan girl is one of many who suffer from hunger in Africa.

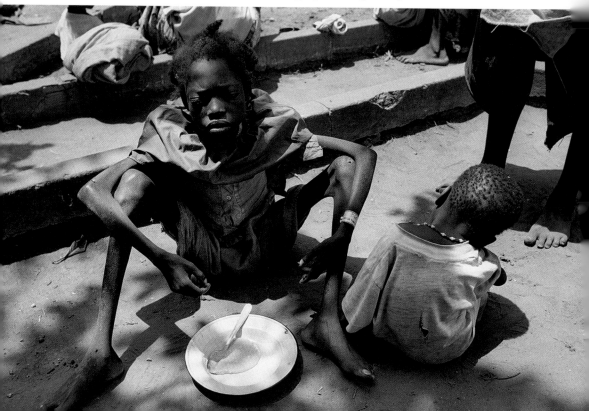

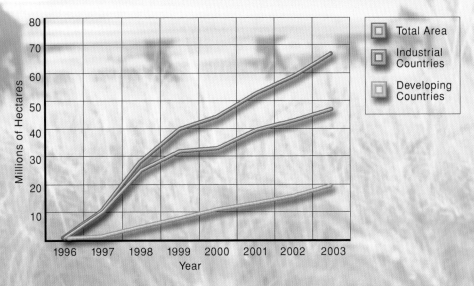

Area Devoted to Genetically Modified Crops

Source: Felicia Wu and William P. Butz, *The Future of Genetically Engineered Crops*. Santa Monica, CA: Rand, 2004.

national companies and small-holder farmers stand to benefit as confirmed by experiences in China and Africa. While the focus has been on benefits to the private sector, programs such as the tissue culture banana project in some East African countries have demonstrated that biotechnology can have a positive impact on hunger, malnutrition and poverty. In some cases, rural farm incomes have tripled as a result of biotech techniques.

The question then arises: Should the agricultural sector remain unchanged while every other aspect of life on the continent is changing? The anti-biotech lobby asserts that the continent needs to be protected from big multinational biotech companies. This often Euro-centric view is founded on two premises: that Africa has no expertise to make an informed decision and that the continent should focus on organic farming. These perspectives, even if well intended, do not represent the African scientists' view. . . .

Issues of Trade and Safety

Did Zambia have any valid reasons for rejecting GM food? No. But Zambia did have valid reasons for asking questions about trade and

Source: Duffy. © 2000 by King Features Syndicate. Reproduced by permission.

food safety issues. First, brushing aside the issue of trade with the European Union (EU) is simplistic. But total rejection of GM food is equally simplistic. For historical, political and economic reasons, Africa's main trading partner is Europe. In view of the EU moratorium on GM food, African countries that favor the use of GM crops must put on their thinking caps and decide how best to deal with the trade issue. My country, Kenya, has discovered that in the last five years, neighboring Uganda has become our largest trading partner, overtaking Britain. Regionally, the Common Market for Eastern and Southern Africa has recently surpassed the EU as Kenya's main trading bloc. These are relevant lessons for Zambia.

The second issue is one of safety. As a scientist, who has been in the lab and have been involved in biotechnology for over 10 years, I can confirm that rigorous testing takes place to ensure GM foods are safe. Indeed, a number of the foods that we eat would fail miserably if passed through the rigor of GM food testing. There are no proven dangers from GM foods, although even pro-GM scientists would agree there are always potential dangers. Mobile phone technology is spreading like wild fire in Africa, despite the alleged danger of cancer-causing effects. Should we stop using cell phones? The simple answer is that the benefits far outweigh any potential dangers.

The needs of Africa and Europe are different. Europe has surplus food and does not experience hunger, mass starvation and death on the scale we frequently and sadly witness in Africa. The priority of Africa is to feed her people with safe foods and to sustain agricultural production and the environment. Based on what is happening on the continent, it is a foregone conclusion that biotechnology is causing a silent revolution in Africa. Farmers have embraced the new technology because it makes them more efficient, protecting—or increasing—yields and reducing their reliance on chemicals. . . .

A Major Impact

Critics of biotechnology claim that Africa has no chance to benefit from biotechnology, and that Africa will only be exploited by multinationals. On the contrary, small-scale farmers in Africa have benefited by using hybrid seeds from local and multinational companies, and transgenic seeds in effect are simply an added-value improvement to these hybrids. Local farmers are benefiting from tissue-culture technologies for banana, sugar cane, pyrethrum, cassava and other crops. There is every reason to believe they will also benefit from the crop-protection transgenic technologies in the pipeline for banana, such as sigatoka, the disease-resistant transgenic variety now ready for field trials. Virus- and pest-resistant transgenic sugar cane technologies are being developed in countries such as Mauritius, South Africa and Egypt.

> ## FAST FACT
>
> According to the International Service of Agri-Biotech Applications, more than one-quarter (27%) of the world's genetically engineered crop area in 2002, equivalent to 39.5 million acres, was located in developing countries.

Kenya—which is currently drafting laws to govern GM foods—has opted to build capacity in every area necessary to adopt biotechnology, while moving with care. We appreciate that there could be potential dangers, but we also know very well the benefits. For example, let's look at the effect of GM technology on three important crops in Africa.

Crop	World (Ave. Yield: tonnes per hectare)	Africa (Ave. Yield: tonnes per hectare)
Maize	4.1	1.7
Sweet potatoes	14.7	4.8
Bananas	48.1	6.0

As is clearly evident, with GM technology Africa can quadruple its maize output, more than triple sweet potato output and increase banana output by eight times. Anybody who cares about hunger should be interested in this technology. It is my considered opinion that biotechnology is already having a major impact on agricultural and public policies in Africa from a continental level. . . .

We may have missed the green revolution, which helped Asia and Latin America achieve self-sufficiency in food production, but we cannot afford to be excluded or to miss another major global technological revolution. The people of Africa cannot wait for others to debate the merits of biotechnology—and we look to America and other developed nations to help us allocate technologies that can prevent suffering and starvation.

EVALUATING THE AUTHORS' ARGUMENTS:

In the viewpoint you just read Florence Wambugu argues that Africans support the use of agricultural biotechnology. In the next viewpoint, Anuradha Mittal insists that Third World farmers, including African farmers, oppose the use of genetically engineered crops. Which author is more persuasive on this point, and why?

Genetically Modified Crops Will Not Help Developing Nations

Anuradha Mittal

> *"Hunger in the Third World is a complex phenomenon and not likely to be reversed by genetically engineered (GE) crops."*

Anuradha Mittal is the codirector of the Institute for Food and Development Policy, popularly known as Food First, an organization that seeks solutions to hunger and poverty around the world. The following viewpoint is an excerpt from a speech Mittal delivered to a forum sponsored by CropLife International, an organization that represents the plant science industry and promotes the use of genetic engineering in agriculture. The topic of the forum was "social morality" and agricultural biotechnology.

In her viewpoint Mittal suggests that the biotechnology industry has violated social morality in various ways. For example, she charges that the industry has been dishonest in its claims about the ability of genetically engineered foods to end hunger and starvation in the developing world. She contends that contrary to the claims of the biotech industry, hunger is not caused by a shortage of food but rather by poverty and by government policies that keep food out of the hands of those who need it. These problems will not be solved by the increased use of agricultural biotechnology. In addition, she claims that the biotechnology industry, aided by Western governments, has attempted to coerce developing nations to grow genetically engineered crops despite the risks they pose to human health and the environment.

AS YOU READ, CONSIDER THE FOLLOWING QUESTIONS:
1. How many pounds of food are available per person, according to Mittal?
2. How did Tony Hall respond to Zambia's refusal to accept GE corn, according to the author? And why was this response ironic?
3. What labor practices of biotech companies does Mittal oppose?

Speaking at a graduation ceremony at the US Coast Guard academy, Mr. [George W.] Bush asserted that Europe's refusal to allow GE foods into their markets had discouraged Third World countries from using this technology and thus undermined efforts to end hunger in Africa. A week before, his administration had filed a suit at the World Trade Organization (WTO) to force Europe to lift its moratorium on GM foods.

In a press release, CropLife America commended the US decision, and Isi Siddiqui, Vice President of CropLife America, was quoted as saying, "The EU's illegal moratorium had a negative ripple effect of creeping regulations which have resulted in denying food to starving people."

Hunger Is Complex

Social morality requires that instead of corporate PR campaigns based on "poor washing," conferring legitimacy and preventing debate over a policy by spurious suggestion that the poor will benefit from it, we should acknowledge that we live with the paradox of hunger amidst plenty. According to our research at Food First (www.foodfirst.org), abundance, not scarcity, best describes the world's food supply. Enough wheat, rice and other grains are produced to provide every human being with 3,500 calories a day. That doesn't even count many other commonly eaten foods—vegetables, beans, nuts, root crops, fruits, grass fed meats, and fish. Enough food is available to provide at least 4.3 pounds of food per person a day worldwide: 2.5 pounds of grain, beans and nuts, about a pound of fruits and vegetables, and nearly another pound of meat, milk and eggs—enough to make most people fat! It is not the shortage of food production, but poverty that keeps people hungry.

My country, India, home to over 350 million hungry people, is the third largest producer of food in the world. In 2000, while starvation deaths were reported from across the country, the granaries of the Food Corporation of India (FCI) were overflowing with 80 million tons of excess food grains, and the government of India was unable to find enough export markets. They even contemplated dumping rat infested grain into the sea. This year [2003], India has over 40 millions tons of excess food grains, yet millions starve.

Some farmers in the developing world, like these rice farmers in China, remain wary of the use of genetically engineered crops.

Hunger in the Third World is a complex phenomenon and not likely to be reversed by genetically engineered (GE) crops. Almost 78% of countries that report child malnutrition are food exporting countries. Over a third of the grain grown in the developing world is destined for livestock which in turn is eaten by consumers in wealthy countries. Hunger has nothing to do with some deficit of food production, but a shortage of people's purchasing power! Given this state of affairs, social morality demands the industry give a better rationale for their promotion of GE crops in the Third World than hunger. . . .

When Zambia refused GE corn food aid from the United States, it failed to get requested support to promote and distribute cassava, a traditional food. "Better dead than GM fed?" was the derisive response of the *Economist* magazine. Tony Hall, the U.S. ambassador to UN food agencies went a step further, equating Zambia's rejection to a crime against humanity. He claimed, "All of it has passed U.S. food safety and environmental impact testing—the most rigorous in the world. For this reason we do not need to separate genetically modified (GM) and non GM foods." It seemed ludicrous to Hall, a representative of the bastion of democracy and social morality, that a debate should even be allowed in African nations over the health and environmental risks posed by GE crops. . . .

> **FAST FACT**
>
> According to Greenpeace, in Latin America, 80 percent of agricultural land is in the hands of 20 percent of the farmers; the other 20 percent of the land is in the hands of the remaining 80 percent.

Real aid was not offered to Zambia; instead, U.S. $51 million was given as a loan to Zambia for the private sector to import GE corn from the U.S. When it was imported, Zambia was not informed that it was contaminated, nor did the U.S. seek its prior consent to ship GE corn. While the U.S. accused Zambia of starving its people, offers of GE free corn came in from India, China, Kenya, Tanzania, and Uganda. Japan actually provided GE free corn food aid.

The Third World Opposes GE Crops

Social morality would require an acknowledgement that not just Africa, but the Third World has largely united against U.S.-pushed GM crops,

Mary Robbins, the UN High Commissioner for Human Rights, answers questions at a UN Food and Agriculture Organization (FAO) antihunger summit.

opting instead for self-sufficiency. Internal debate within Third World nations pits mostly U.S. trained technocrats, seduced by technological fixes, against farmers and consumers who are overwhelmingly saying no to GE crops. In 1998 all African delegates (except South Africa) to the FAO [UN Food and Agriculture Organization] negotiations on the International Undertaking for Plant Genetic Resources released a statement, "Let the Nature's Harvest Continue," in response to a publicity campaign in European newspapers trying to convince the readers that the world needs GE foods to feed the hungry. Organized and financed by Monsanto, that campaign was titled, "Let the Harvest Begin." In their statement, the African delegates objected "to the use of the image of the poor and hungry by corporations to push a technology that is neither safe, environmentally friendly, nor economically beneficial to us."

The farmers' movement in India has found a new use for an old slogan of the Indian liberation struggle. They reissued the "Quit India" ultimatum, this time to corporations like Monsanto, and under their "Cremate Monsanto" they have burned field trials of GE crops, which were planted against their wishes. . . .

What Social Morality Requires

If industry cared about social morality, it would recognize that Monsanto and its Indian subsidiary employ some 17,000 Indian children for 50 cents a day, who get no education. More than 11,000 work for Syngenta, Advanta, and Proagro. Social morality would question U.S. Senator [Bill] Frist, whose AIDS bill suggests medical blackmail in the form of withholding AIDS medications from African nations if they refuse GE food aid. Social morality would question USAID [U.S. Agency for International Development], who has advised that the USDA [U.S. Department of Agriculture] report any Third World nations who refuse GE food aid so other assistance can be turned off to them as punishment. Social morality would question corporations who claim that GM foods pose no threats, since they are the same as old varieties, while they rush to patent offices to secure patents of innovation, claiming they are different.

It would question corporations like Monsanto who claim genetic engineering offers new agronomical benefits to farmers. Do they perhaps mean benefits from their lawsuit against over 2,000 farmers in the U.S. and Canada for patent infringement? It would question Monsanto's monopoly on GE soy, a patent on all varieties of GM soy valid until 2014. It would question the top two chemical companies who control 40% of the global market. And question Monsanto who seeks royalties on GE soy illegally planted in Brazil. . . .

This is not news to you [i.e., CropLife International]. Industry can choose to dismiss concerns around safety, environmental risks, Intellectual Property Rights, and corporate personhood. Industry might choose to ridicule the opposition to GE foods. But industry does know that dissent is growing, and is fueled by the corporate attack on seeds, which are humanity's heritage, and has resorted to tactics that defy all principles of social morality and threaten the food security of the Third World. Dupont and Monsanto are spending millions buying up local seed companies in their effort to control our food system. Seeds are the first link of the food chain. Control of the seed is control of the food system.

Millions of Indian children go hungry every year despite the fact that India has ample food to feed them.

Industry fears the truth—and the truth is that it is losing. Monsanto suffered a loss of 20% in stocks price last year [2002]. This year it has already reported a loss of 15%. It is time to accept that food and agriculture are sacred for farmers and communities in the Third World. This is about our culture, our life and our livelihoods, and we are not about to surrender it to corporations to boost their profits. And as far as social morality is concerned, as long as corporate efforts gag the voices of the poor, indigenous people, and the campesinos [native Latin American farmers], the biotech industry cannot offer us an agricultural system which is just, sustainable, or honorable.

EVALUATING THE AUTHOR'S ARGUMENTS:

The viewpoint you just read was excerpted from a speech delivered at a forum sponsored by CropLife International. Anuradha Mittal repeatedly invokes CropLife's own phrase, "social morality," against the very companies CropLife represents. Do you think this rhetorical technique is successful? That is, does it strengthen or weaken the author's criticisms of the biotechnology industry? Explain.

The Genetic Engineering of Animals Can Benefit Society

Lester Crawford

> *"The FDA has ample experience . . . to evaluate products manufactured with the help of transgenic animals."*

Lester Crawford is the commissioner of the U.S. Food and Drug Administration (FDA), the government agency that oversees the safety of America's food and drug supply. In the following viewpoint he contends that applying genetic engineering technology to animals can lead to the production of useful products for food, science, and medicine. For example, cows can be genetically engineered to produce different kinds of milk, and fish can be genetically altered to be more nutritious. In addition, bioengineered pigs and rats can serve as models for science; because these animals are in some ways similar to humans, scientists can use them to study human diseases and develop treatments for them. Animals can also be genetically engineered to produce proteins in their milk, semen, or blood that can be used in medicines to treat human diseases. While Crawford concedes there are risks associated with genetically engineering animals, he insists that the FDA can ensure that the technology is developed safely.

Lester Crawford, "Reaping the Biotech Harvest," *American Enterprise*, March 2004.

AS YOU READ, CONSIDER THE FOLLOWING QUESTIONS:
1. Why is it better to produce proteins for human medicines in animals rather than in cell cultures, plants, or microorganisms, according to Crawford?
2. What types of genetically engineered mosquitoes and mites are being developed, as reported by the author?
3. What are "pleiotropic effects," as defined by Crawford?

Today's biotechnology includes the use of genetically modified animals in medicine; in the production of special foods, human drugs, and medical devices; in the development of animal and industrial products; and in insect-based pest and disease control. Bioengineered animals are now commonly used for the exploration of medical questions that cannot be readily studied otherwise, such as the mechanisms of both normal physiology and disease in humans and animals. Special pigs, for example, are often used to model human disease, because the size and function of their organs are similar to those of humans. One example is a pig strain bioengineered to test retinitis pigmentosa, a progressive disease that begins with night blindness, and affects between 100,000 and 400,000 people in the U.S. The pig model is intended to help develop drugs to slow the onset and progression of the disease.

Other bioengineered laboratory models include rodents, to study how inborn errors cause disease. Insects and fish are also employed to study disease or population dynamics. Drosophila melanogaster, the common fruit fly some of us remember from our college days, is often bioengineered as a model for developmental studies. Transgenic zebrafish and Amazon mollies are used to study effects of ultraviolet irradiation on melanomas.

Bioengineered Animals for Food and Medicine

More familiar—and controversial—is the use of bioengineered animals to produce certain foods and medical products. Cows can be genetically engineered to make several kinds of specialized milk. They can produce milk with lower levels of a protein that may make the milk more suitable for up to 6 percent of U.S. infants and others allergic to regular cow milk. They can also produce milk that's more digestible for people who are lactose intolerant; milk that has more naturally occurring antimicrobial enzymes, which increase the milk's shelf life; and milk with altered proteins such as caseins, or with lower water content, which facilitates cheese production. Fish can also be modified to make them more nutritious. One example is the modification of rainbow trout to increase the amount of their omega-3 fatty acids, which can help prevent heart attacks. Within the next few years, we're likely to see many more such products.

Genetic engineering can also develop animals capable of producing therapeutic proteins. In general, these proteins will be produced in the milk of cows, sheep, or goats; in chicken eggs; in the semen of swine; or in blood of various large farm species. The advantage of producing these proteins in animals—rather than in cell or tissue cultures, plants, or microorganisms—is significant. The proteins are better adapted to human use, and the yields are higher. In addition, the post-development costs are lower, because raising a herd of dairy cows is cheaper than building and maintaining a bioreactor facility.

The production of the protein alpha-1-antitrypsin in sheep's milk is a good example. This is a human blood protein used to treat hereditary

By creating genetically modified animals, such as this obese mouse, researchers hope to develop cures for human ailments.

emphysema, cystic fibrosis, and chronic obstructive pulmonary disease, believed to affect more than 200,000 people in the U.S. and Europe. This product is already in clinical trials in Europe. Bioengineered animals could also be useful as a source of transplant organs and for medical products such as spider silk made from goat's milk for sturdy sutures, as replacement tendons, or even for bulletproof vests. Genetic engineering of animals is also being used to create faster-growing, bigger, nutrition-enhanced, or disease-resistant salmon, shellfish, pigs, and many other animals. Several approaches are being investigated to modify mosquitoes so they can't spread malaria or certain fevers. There are also techniques that enhance the predatory behavior of certain mites against others that infest plants, which could reduce the use of pesticides.

Genetically engineered fish that grow faster and larger than ordinary fish may soon be available in the marketplace.

Acknowledging the Risks

The Food and Drug Administration [FDA] is familiar with the risks of biotechnology. We are aware that using genetically altered animals for food raises serious safety concerns that must be addressed through rigorous, science-based analysis. Bioactive compounds are a good example. They include growth hormones, proteins that aid in resisting disease, and even proteins of pharmaceutical interest. If these proteins are present in edible tissues of transgenic animals, they might pose a food safety risk.

Allergic reactions are another concern. The risk of adverse reactions is raised whenever foods contain new proteins from genetically modified organisms, regardless of whether their source is an animal, plant, or microorganism such as yeast or bacteria.

When it comes to technologies that use viral sequences to introduce new genes, we must consider the possibility that a viral vector used to create some desired trait could recombine with existing viruses in the animal and create a new pathogen. Yet another hazard may arise when the insertion of a gene produces unintended adverse outcomes, known as "pleiotropic effects." These result from the disruption of a cell's normal function, and may lead to cell death. There is also the possibility that biotech products are mishandled through human negligence or error.

> ## FAST FACT
>
> In the spring of 2005, researchers in Japan and the United States announced the results of a study that found no significant differences between the milk and beef derived from cloned cows and cows produced with traditional breeding methods. The U.S. Food and Drug Administration has not approved the sale of food from cloned animals.

The FDA's Oversight

How will the FDA cope with the large-scale introduction of products as technologically advanced, highly beneficial, and yet potentially risky as genetically altered animals? We have over a decade of experience in examining more than 50 edible products made from genetically modified plants. The FDA also has a century long record of determining food safety.

Our goal is to make sure that a new product is as safe as its natural counterpart. The FDA has ample experience, as well as legal authority

'Wow!'

Source: Reproduced by permission of *The Spectator*.

and guidance, for ensuring the safety and effectiveness of drugs, biological medications, and medical devices, and it would use these same resources to evaluate products manufactured with the help of transgenic animals.

But what about other concerns, including the critical question whether, and to what extent, the safety of the environment would be put at risk by genetically altered animals? And what about risks to the animals themselves? The FDA has yet to answer these questions by approving or disapproving the application for marketing of any transgenic animal.

Not much is known about the FDA's vigorous efforts to help ensure the safety of biotechnology. Two years ago [in 2002] we requested that animal cloners withhold any food products made from clones and their progeny until the FDA evaluates potential safety issues. Just like human twins who share the same genome, animal clones are not exact copies, and we need time to collect data for informed decisions about the potential risks these animals may pose to other animals or, as a source of food, to people. We are now finishing food consumption and animal health risk assessments for animal clones, and plan to make them available for public comment. The FDA has also commissioned the National Academy of Sciences to review potential risks of products of genetically modified animals.

The ultimate success of G.M. products is crucially dependent on transparency and producers' communication with the media and the public. The FDA is committed to ensuring that biotech products are safe and that alarming talk about "Frankenfood" recognized as idle talk that can only do damage.

EVALUATING THE AUTHORS' ARGUMENTS:

Lester Crawford is the commissioner of the Food and Drug Administration, a government agency that monitors the safety of the nation's foods and medicines. The author of the next viewpoint, Karen Hirsch, is the managing editor of a magazine devoted to the protection of animals. How does knowing the backgrounds of these two authors affect your evaluation of their viewpoints? Are you predisposed to agree with either of the authors in advance? Are you inclined to trust Crawford more or less than Hirsch? Explain your answers.

The Genetic Engineering of Animals Is Harmful

Karen Hirsch

"Few people . . . are aware of how biotech practices affect animals."

Karen Hirsch is the managing editor of *Animal Issues,* a magazine published by the Animal Protection Institute, an organization that advocates the protection of animals from cruelty and exploitation. In the following viewpoint, she argues that genetic engineering of animals is harmful to animals and poses risks to humans and the environment. The use of biotechnology in agriculture, she contends, simply adds to the animal cruelty already existing on today's factory farms. Moreover, she maintains, grotesque genetic experiments are being conducted on animals in the name of science and medicine. These experiments often result in deformities and physical suffering in animals while providing no useful applications.

AS YOU READ, CONSIDER THE FOLLOWING QUESTIONS:

1. What risks are posed by genetically engineered fish, according to Hirsch?
2. What are "biobugs," as described by the author?
3. What are the risks of "biopharming," according to Hirsch?

Environmental advocates have been successful at publicizing their concerns about biotech processes, particularly genetic engineering. Polls reveal that a majority of Americans worry about the effect so-called "Frankenfoods" may have on the environment, the food supply, and human health. Few people, however, are aware of how biotech practices affect animals. . . .

Animals in Biotech Agriculture

One of the most appalling ways in which biotechnology affects animals is in agriculture. Scientists and corporations are hard at work trying to "perfect" methods by which animals are exploited for food. As if existing industry conditions weren't sufficiently horrific, meat producers are now, as author Matthew Scully puts it, "redesigning the animal to suit the factory farm."

Farm animals are subjected to a wide variety of abuses, including genetic modification, cloning, and the forced ingestion of powerful hormones and antibiotics—all to increase yields and efficiency and,

A Wisconsin dairy farmer uses bovine growth hormone to increase the milk production of his cows.

therefore, the profits of food manufacturers. Some high-tech projects currently in the works would seem laughably absurd if they weren't frighteningly real: cows engineered to produce more tender, easy-to-cut flesh; pigs modified to be less stressed by the slaughterhouse; goats injected with rat or even human genes in an effort to make tastier milk. All of these practices raise serious ethical and health concerns. . . .

Cloning is another developing technology enthusiastically embraced by the meat industry. In January of this year [2003], an unnamed

Genetically engineered mice are frequently used in medical studies.

Canadian company applied for government permission to begin selling meat derived from cloned animals; a decision was pending at press time. Animals cloned in laboratories have consistently experienced serious physical and developmental problems. Many grow abnormally large in utero, develop congenital anomalies, and die before or soon after birth. The genetic uniformity of cloned animals also makes them susceptible to painful diseases and deformities. In addition, questions still remain regarding the safety of meat derived from cloned animals.

GE Fish

While restaurants offering cloned-cow-burgers may remain years away, genetically-engineered (GE) fish could soon be served on a plate near you. Currently, there are 35 species of GE fish at various stages of development around the world. These animals are manipulated at a cellular level to contain a desired trait—most commonly, the ability to grow anywhere from two to thirty times faster than their natural counterparts.

Many scientists believe that GE fish pose significant environmental and health threats. A recent Purdue University study indicated that if GE fish escaped into open waters (as farm-raised fish often do), they would likely outcompete their wild counterparts for food and mates. Because offspring of GE fish have high mortality rates due to the impacts of added genetic material, the result of such a scenario could be the extinction of the native species within a few generations.

Researchers have also raised concerns about the potential toxicity, allergenic properties, and aquaculture disease rates of GE fish. At press time, the U.S. Food and Drug Administration (FDA) was considering an application from a Massachusetts company, Aqua Bounty Farms,

> ## FAST FACT
>
> The Board on Agriculture and Natural Resources (BANR) reports that a pig was genetically engineered with a human growth hormone in order to alter its growth rate and decrease its fat content. According to the BANR, "The pigs were plagued by a variety of physical problems, including diarrhea, mammary development in males, lethargy, arthritis, lameness, skin and eye problems, loss of libido, and disruption of estrous cycles." Seventeen of the nineteen pigs died within the first year.

to market fast-growing GE salmon for human consumption. Experts worry that the FDA, which has the authority to regulate such fish under the rules covering drugs for animals, is ill-equipped to adequately assess potential environmental damage these new breeds may cause. . . .

Genetic Animal Experiments

Moving beyond the grocery store shelves, we find that animals are also the subject of manipulation and abuse in the name of science. . . .

Among the odd and sometimes gruesome "accomplishments" of researchers: animals that glow in the dark; animals deliberately inflicted with painful deformities; and animals that are hybrids of two or more species. Recently, "biobugs" were the talk of the scientific town. These engineered insects were manipulated for a variety of human uses, including the delivery of pesticides to crops and of vaccinations to humans that they bite. Researchers and ethicists have also been debating the value of the "humouse" (a mouse-human hybrid), and a Stanford University project in which a mouse was injected with millions of human brain cells.

FAST FACT

In 2004 GloFish became the first genetically engineered animal to be sold to the public. These ornamental fish contain a gene from a sea anemone, which causes them to glow a brilliant red color when under black light.

Much of the work in laboratories focuses on the creation of transgenic animals, who have had genetic material from other species introduced into their bodies during embryonic development. This process often amplifies particular traits or conditions not normally found in unaltered animals. Transgenic animals have been created to study disease susceptibility, growth rates, and other issues, or out of what appears to be little more than curiosity—research for research's sake.

Examples of transgenic animals created to date include catfish injected with moth genes to enhance resistance to bacteria; goats with the ability to produce spider silk; and pigs who grow to outsized proportions thanks to the human growth hormones in their systems. In his book *Beyond Evolution,* Dr. Michael W. Fox notes that "thousands of varieties of transgenic animals have been created, and in many instances mortality is high and suffering is considerable." These study "participants" are often forced to live out their days in sterile, isolated environments and experience physical deformities, psychological distress, and other problems.

Closely related to transgenics are hybrid, or chimeric, animals, which are the result of the genetic blending of two unrelated species. The first such creature was a sheep-goat chimera concocted in a British laboratory in 1984. According to Richard Heinberg, author of *Cloning the Buddha*, the point of the experiment was to see if the species barrier could be broken in pregnancy. Apparently, this barrier is permeable—a fact of dubious utility learned only through the suffering of thousands of sentient test subjects.

Using Animals for Medicine

Another increasingly popular use of animals is as living pharmaceutical factories. In "biopharming," scientists manipulate animals on a cellular and genetic level so that they secrete proteins and other substances that may have research applications or medicinal properties. Examples of so-called "pharm" animals include rabbits who produce bone-building proteins in their milk; pigs who secrete a human hemoglobin substitute;

"HEY, MOM! YOU SURE THERE ARE NO SIDE EFFECTS FROM CLONED FOOD?!"

Source: Payne. © 2003 by the *Detroit News*. Reproduced by permission of United Feature Syndicate, Inc.

and mice who make human growth hormone in their urinary bladder cells. The National Academy of Sciences reports that these animals often suffer from "pathologies and other severe systemic effects" when forced to produce such proteins. In addition to the obvious ethical and humane concerns that arise from biopharming, the actual utility of the experiments is questionable. Biopharmed product safety is an enormous concern, largely because of the risk of allergic reactions if such substances are used in humans.

Similar safety concerns exist about xenotransplantation, or the use of animal organs, cells, and tissues in humans. Increasingly, many species of animal are being viewed as "biomachines," mere factories for replacement body parts. API [the Animal Protection Institute] has long opposed this practice, and works to shape policy on the issue through publications, conference presentations, and participation on the federal Department of Health and Human Services' Secretary's Advisory Commission on Xenotransplantation. . . .

Advocating for Animals

Animal advocates must strive to be educated consumers and citizens. We must use compassion and caution to guide us in what we purchase and what we eat. Our voices must be heard when the FDA prepares its guidelines for cloning and transgenic animals. . . . We must tell our legislators what we think as they consider laws related to genetic engineering. And we must grapple with our own conflicted feelings about technology. It is a force that touches our lives in countless ways every day, and which can be positive and beneficial or dangerous and inhumane, depending on who benefits and who suffers.

EVALUATING THE AUTHORS' ARGUMENTS:

After reading the viewpoints by Crawford and Hirsch, do you believe animals should be genetically engineered even if animals are harmed in the process? Explain your reasoning.

agricultural biotechnology: The use of genetic engineering on plants and animals to produce food and medicines.

biotechnology, or **biotech:** A broad term that can include genetic engineering, reproductive technology, and the use of genetic technology to address environmental problems and to develop agricultural products and medicines.

Bt: Abbreviation for the bacterium *Bacillus thuringiensis.* **Transgenic** Bt crops have a **gene** from the bacterium that causes them to produce a common agricultural insecticide.

designer baby: A term commonly used in discussions of genetic enhancement. Designer babies are the hypothetical children of the future genetically engineered to possess desirable traits such as improved intelligence or athletic ability.

DNA (deoxyribonucleic acid): The molecule that is the basic genetic material found in all living things.

eugenics: The science of improving a breed or species, especially the human species, either through genetic engineering or by encouraging reproduction by persons presumed to have desirable genetic traits.

gene: A specialized segment of **DNA** whose sequence encodes the structure of a **protein**; genes are responsible for all the inherited characteristics of an organism.

gene flow: The movement of genes from one breeding population to another by means of migration.

gene splicing: Inserting genetic material from one species into that of another in order to introduce a desired trait into the newly created organism.

gene therapy: The treatment of inheritable diseases through the insertion of healthy genes to replace defective ones. There are two types of gene therapy: **Somatic gene therapy** and **germ line therapy.**

genetically engineered food: Food that contains ingredients from **genetically engineered organisms.**

genetically engineered organism, also known as **genetically modified organism:** Plants or animals that have been altered by means of genetic engineering.

genetic enhancement: The theoretical use of genetic engineering technology not to cure diseases but to produce humans with traits that are believed to be desirable, such as an extended life span, superior intelligence, or greater height.

genetic screening: The testing of individuals, fetuses, embryos, or sperm or egg cells for genetic traits or for abnormalities, including mutations associated with genetic diseases.

genome: The complete set of **genes** in an organism.

germ line therapy, also called **germ line engineering:** Treating genetic diseases or disorders by altering genes in a reproductive cell, such as a sperm or egg cell. Because this type of gene therapy, so far only theoretical, would make genetic changes to reproductive cells, those changes would be transmitted to all subsequent generations, thus causing irreversible changes to the human gene pool.

Green Revolution: The large increase in crop productivity in the 1960s and 1970s resulting in part from the application of genetic science to agriculture.

hectare: A unit of area measure in the metric system. One hectare equals 2.47 square acres.

inheritable genetic modification: Any form of genetic engineering that results in altered genetic traits that will be passed on to future generations, including **germ line therapy** and **genetic enhancement.**

in vitro fertilization: An assisted reproductive technology in which a woman's eggs are removed from her womb and fertilized in a laboratory. The resulting embryos are then implanted in the woman's womb and allowed to develop until birth.

precautionary principle: The theory that if an action might cause serious harm to the environment, even if that harm cannot be definitively proven, the action should not be taken.

protein: A broad term used to describe many of the organic molecules that constitute a large portion of the mass of every organism; each gene in an organism encodes one protein.

pre-implantation genetic screening and selection: The screening of embryos produced through **in vitro fertilization** for genetic diseases and traits. Embryos with the desired characteristics (such as the preferred sex) are selected for implantation in the womb whereas those without such traits—as well as those with genetic diseases—are rejected.

recombinant DNA: A segment of DNA that includes DNA from different sources, including different species.

recombinant DNA technology: The procedures used to manipulate and recombine DNA—that is, to perform genetic engineering.

somatic gene therapy: A form of gene therapy in which healthy genes are inserted into the somatic, or body, cells of a person with a genetic disease or disorder. Because only the somatic cells, and not the sex cells, are affected, the genetic changes are not passed on to the patient's offspring.

transgenic: Having genetic material that was introduced from another species.

FACTS ABOUT GENETIC ENGINEERING

Editor's Note: These facts can be used in reports or papers to reinforce or add credibility when making important points or claims.

Human Genetic Engineering

Somatic gene therapy, the use of genetic technology to treat individuals with genetic disorders, has been attempted with mixed success. Germ line therapy, which would make changes that are passed on to future generations, has not yet been attempted on humans, although it has been practiced on animals since the 1980s.

Genetic enhancement, using genetic engineering to improve the human race or to "design" babies with "preferable" traits such as improved intelligence or increased height, has not yet been attempted.

All human gene therapy research must be approved by the U.S. Food and Drug Administration.

The first human-to-human genetic transfer occurred in 1989, when researchers inserted genes into a cancer patient in an attempt to track tumor-fighting immune system cells. Although the experiment did not affect the patient's cancer (nor was it intended to), it proved that genes could be transferred without harming the patient.

The first gene therapy experiment took place in 1990, when a four-year-old girl successfully received treatment for adenosine deaminase (ADA) deficiency, a condition that results in a faulty immune system. Some of her blood was drawn, healthy ADA genes were added to it, and the blood was returned to her body.

In 1999 eighteen-year-old Jesse Gelsinger died during a gene therapy experiment for the disease ornithine transcarbamylase (OTC), which impairs the liver's ability to remove ammonia from the bloodstream. Gelsinger's death prompted a reevaluation of the regulation of gene therapy research.

In 2003, researchers in France halted a gene therapy trial for babies born with immune system deficiencies after two of the ten patients developed leukemia. The U.S. Food and Drug Administration halted twenty-seven similar studies.

Hundreds of gene therapy trials are currently being conducted around the world.

Genetic Engineering of Plants and Animals

In agriculture, genetic engineering involves the manipulation of plant genes in order to create plants with a desired trait, such as resistance to herbicides and pesticides, resistance to environmental stressors such as cold, heat, drought, and salty soils, and increased yields. This process involves inserting genes from a different species—including plant, animal, or even human genes.

Genetically modified crops that are commonly grown around the world include soybean, corn, canola, and cotton.

As of 2003, eighteen countries were growing genetically engineered crops. Of these, the United States had the most such crops, with 105.7 million acres, making up 63 percent of U.S. farmlands.

The Food and Drug Administration requires testing and labeling of genetically engineered food products that have a significantly altered nutritional value or that contain a known allergen. Most foods that contain genetically engineered ingredients do not meet this criteria and therefore are unlabeled.

The European Union has banned the growth of genetically modified crops, although in 2004 it made two exceptions to this ban, approving two types of genetically engineered corn.

The European Union requires labels to identify products that contain genetically modified ingredients.

ORGANIZATIONS TO CONTACT

Alliance for Bio-Integrity
2040 Pearl Lane, Suite 2, Fairfield, IA 52556
(206) 888-4852
e-mail: info@biointegrity.org
Web site: www.biointegrity.org

The Alliance for Bio-Integrity is a nonprofit organization that opposes the use of genetic engineering in agriculture and works to educate the public about the dangers of genetically modified foods. Position papers that argue against genetic engineering from legal, religious, and scientific perspectives—including "Why Concerns About Health Risks of Genetically Engineered Food Are Scientifically Justified"—are available on its Web site.

Biotechnology Industry Organization (BIO)
1225 Eye St. NW, Suite 400, Washington, DC 20005
(202) 962-9200
fax: (202) 962-9201
e-mail: info@bio.org
Web site: www.bio.org

BIO represents biotechnology companies, academic institutions, state biotechnology centers, and related organizations that support the use of biotechnology in improving health care, agriculture, efforts to clean up the environment, and other fields. BIO works to educate the public about biotechnology and respond to concerns about the safety of genetic engineering and other technologies. It publishes fact sheets, backgrounders, and position papers on various issues related to genetic engineering, including "Facts and Fiction About Plant and Animal Biotechnology."

Center for Bioethics and Human Dignity (CBHD)
2065 Half Day Rd., Bannockburn, IL 60015
(847) 317-8180
fax: (847) 317-8101

e-mail: info@cbhd.org
Web site: www.cbhd.org

CBHD is an international education center whose purpose is to bring Christian perspectives to bear on contemporary bioethical challenges facing society. Its publications address genetic technologies as well as other topics such as euthanasia and abortion. It publishes the book *Cutting-Edge Bioethics* and the audio CD *The Challenges and Opportunities of Genetic Intervention.* The articles "Biotechnology's Brave New World" and "To Clone or Not to Clone?" are available on its Web site.

Center for Genetics and Society
436 Fourteenth St., Suite 1302, Oakland, CA 94612
(510) 625-0819
fax: (510) 625-0874
Web site: www.genetics-and-society.org

The center is a nonprofit organization that advocates for the responsible use of genetic technology in the areas of health care, human reproduction, and agriculture. It favors a cautious approach, including bans on the use of some genetic technologies that it deems threatening to public safety and human rights. Its Web site contains informational and opinionated articles on human genetic engineering as well as the results of numerous public opinion polls on the topic.

Council for Biotechnology Information
1225 Eye St. NW, Suite 400, Washington, DC 20043-0380
Phone: (202) 467-6565
Web site: http://whybiotech.com

The council is an organization made up of biotechnology companies and trade associations. Its purpose is to promote what its members believe are the benefits of biotechnology in agriculture, industry, science, and health care. Its Web site offers numerous reports and FAQs on various topics, including the environmental and economic effects of genetically engineered crops.

Council for Responsible Genetics (CRG)
5 Upland Rd., Suite 3, Cambridge, MA 02140
(617) 868-0870
fax: (617) 491-5344

e-mail: crg@gene-watch.org

Web site: www.gene-watch.org

CRG is a national nonprofit organization of scientists, public health advocates, and others who promote a comprehensive public interest agenda for biotechnology. Its members work to raise public awareness about genetic discrimination, patenting life forms, food safety, and environmental quality. CRG publishes *GeneWatch* magazine, providing access to current and archived articles on its Web site.

Foundation on Economic Trends (FOET)

1660 L St. NW, Suite 216, Washington, DC 20036

(202) 466-2823

fax (202) 429-9602

e-mail: office@foet.org

Web site: www.foet.org

Founded by science critic and author Jeremy Rifkin, the foundation is a nonprofit organization whose mission is to examine emerging trends in science and technology and their impacts on the environment, the economy, culture, and society. FOET works to educate the public about topics such as gene patenting, commercial eugenics, genetic discrimination, and genetically altered food. Its Web site contains news updates and articles, including "Shopping for Humans" and "Unknown Risks of Genetically Engineered Crops."

Friends of the Earth (FOE)

1717 Massachusetts Ave. NW, Suite 600,

Washington, DC 20036-2002

(877) 843-8687

fax: (202) 783-0444

e-mail: foe@foe.org

Web site: www.foe.org

Founded in San Francisco in 1969 by David Brower, Friends of the Earth is a grassroots organization whose goal is to create a more healthy, just world. FOE members founded the world's largest federation of democratically elected environmental groups, Friends of the Earth International. Among other efforts, FOE conducted lab tests confirming that genetically engineered corn not approved for human consumption was in products on supermarket shelves across the nation. FOE publishes the quarterly newsmagazine *Friends of the Earth,* current and archived issues of which are available on its Web site.

The Hastings Center
21 Malcolm Gordon Rd., Garrison, NY 10524-5555
(845) 424-4040
fax: (845) 424-4545
e-mail: mail@thehastingscenter.org
Web site: www.thehastingscenter.org

The Hastings Center is an independent research institute that explores the medical, ethical, and social ramifications of biomedical advances. The center publishes books, including *Reprogenetics,* the bimonthly *Hastings Center Report,* and the bimonthly newsletter *IRB: Ethics & Human Research.*

National Institutes of Health
National Human Genome Research Institute (NHGRI)
9000 Rockville Pike, Bethesda, MD 20892
(301) 402-0911
fax: (301) 402-2218
Web site: www.nhgri.nih.gov

NIH is the federal government's primary agency for the support of biomedical research. As a division of NIH, NHGRI's mission was to head the Human Genome Project, the federally funded effort to map all human genes, which was completed in April 2003. Now, NHGRI has moved into the genomic era with research aimed at improving human health and fighting disease. Information on the project and relevant articles are available on its Web site.

Organic Consumers Association (OCA)
6101 Cliff Estate Rd., Little Marais, MN 55614
(218) 226-4164
fax: (218) 353-7652
Web site: www.organicconsumers.org

The OCA promotes food safety, organic farming, and sustainable agriculture practices. It provides information on the hazards of genetically engineered food, irradiated food, food grown with toxic sludge fertilizer, mad cow disease, rBGH in milk, and other issues, and organizes boycotts and protests around these issues. It publishes *BioDemocracy News* and its Web site includes many fact sheets and articles on genetically modified foods.

President's Council on Bioethics
1801 Pennsylvania Ave. NW, Suite 700, Washington, DC 20006
(202) 296-4669
e-mail: info@bioethics.gov
Web site: www.bioethics.gov

When the National Bioethics Advisory Commission's charter expired in October 2001, President George W. Bush established the President's Council on Bioethics. It works to protect the rights and welfare of human research subjects and to govern the management and use of genetic information. On its Web site, the council provides access to its report "Beyond Therapy: Biotechnology and the Pursuit of Happiness."

U.S. Department of Agriculture (USDA)
1400 Independence Ave. SW, Washington, DC 20250
Web site: www.nal.usda.gov/bic

The USDA is one of three federal agencies, along with the Environmental Protection Agency (EPA) and the U.S. Food and Drug Administration (FDA), primarily responsible for regulating biotechnology in the United States. The USDA conducts research on the safety of genetically engineered organisms, helps form government policy on agricultural biotechnology, and provides information to the public about these technologies.

FOR FURTHER READING

Books

Britt Bailey and Marc Lappé, eds., *Engineering the Farm: Ethical and Social Aspects of Agricultural Biotechnology.* Washington, DC: Island, 2002. A collection of essays on the ethics and safety of genetically modified foods assembled by two scholars who take a cautionary approach to the technology.

Francis Fukuyama, *Our Posthuman Future: Consequences of the Biotechnology Revolution.* New York: Farrar, Straus and Giroux, 2002. A study of the ethical implications of applying biotechnology to human beings by a renowned conservative scholar who opposes human genetic engineering.

Walter Glannon, *Genes and Future People: Philosophical Issues in Human Genetics.* Boulder, CO: Westview, 2001. An examination of the ethical issues surrounding human genetic engineering. It includes chapters on genetic enhancement and extending the human life span.

Kathleen Hart, *Eating in the Dark: America's Experiment with Genetically Engineered Food.* New York: Pantheon, 2002. An accessible overview by a journalist who is critical of the biotech industry and questions the safety of genetically engineered foods.

Bill McKibben, *Enough: Staying Human in an Engineered Age.* New York: Henry Holt, 2003. A treatise by a well-known opponent of human genetic engineering who believes that using such technology will erode what it means to be human.

Maxwell J. Mehlman, *Wondergenes: Genetic Enhancement and the Future of Society.* Bloomington: Indiana University Press, 2003. An accessible overview of genetic enhancement by a professor of ethics and law who opposes the technology.

Stephen Nottingham, *Eat Your Genes: How Genetcially Modified Food Is Entering Our Diet.* London: Zed, 2003. An overview of genetically modified foods that includes a detailed explanation of the science and assesses the ecological and health risks of its application.

Gregory E. Pence, *Designer Food: Mutant Harvest or Breadbasket of the World?* Lanham, MD: Rowman & Littlefield, 2002. A generally positive overview of genetically modified food by a professor of bioethics. Chapters cover the effects of GE crops on human health, the environment, and world hunger, among other topics.

Gregory E. Pence, ed., *The Ethics of Food: A Reader for the Twenty-First Century.* Lanham, MD: Rowman & Littlefield, 2002. A collection of essays on the ethical issues related to food. It includes essays both for and against genetically modified foods.

Ted Peters, *Playing God? Genetic Determinism and Human Freedom.* New York: Routledge, 2003. An overview of the ethics of genetic technology by a professor of theology. He concludes that using genetic science to build a better future is consistent with religious belief.

Michael Ruse and David Castle, eds., *Genetically Modified Foods: Debating Biotechnology.* Amherst, NY: Prometheus, 2002. A selection of essays on the ethical, safety, environmental, and legal issues raised by genetically modified foods.

Brian Tokar, ed., *Redesigning Life? The Worldwide Challenge to Genetic Engineering.* London: Zed, 2001. A collection of essays by opponents of both genetic engineered foods and the genetic engineering of humans.

Periodicals and Reports

American Enterprise, March 2004. Entire issue on genetic engineering. (www.taemag.com).

Eric Baard, "Supertots and Frankenkids," *Village Voice,* April 23–29, 2003.

Ronald Bailey, "Bioengineering Made Simple," Reason Online, July 9, 2003. (www.reason.com).

Ronald Bailey, "Dr. Strangelunch, or: Why We Should Stop Worrying and Love Genetically Modified Food," Reason Online, January 2001.

Ronald Bailey, "Is Freedom Just Another Word for Random Genes?" Reason Online, April 2, 2003.

Charles M. Benbrook, "Sowing Seeds of Destruction," *New York Times,* July 11, 2003.

Jason Best, "The Splice Age," *OnEarth,* Winter 2003.

British Medical Association, "Genetically Modified Foods and Health: A Second Interim Statement," March 2004. (www.bma.org.uk).

Shannon Brownlee, "Designer Babies," *Washington Monthly,* March 2002.

Austin Dacey, "The New Perfectionism," *Free Inquiry,* June/July 2004.

Sally Deneen, "Food Fight," *E Magazine,* July/August 2003.

Dinesh D'Souza, "Staying Human: The Danger of Techno-Utopia," *National Review,* January 22, 2001.

George Dvorsky, "Thinking Outside the Gene," Betterhumans.com, January 5, 2004. (www.betterhumans.com).

Zac Goldsmith, "Science? The Public Is Right to Smell a Rat," *(London) Independent Sunday,* June 29, 2003.

Leon R. Kass, "The Age of Genetic Technology Arrives," *American Spectator,* November/December 2002.

William Kristol, "The Future Is Now, II," *Weekly Standard,* April 15, 2002.

Stephen Leahy, "Biotech Hope and Hype," *Maclean's,* September 30, 2002.

Bill McKibben, "Keep Us Human," *Los Angeles Times,* April 14, 2003.

Bill McKibben, "A Threat to Our Coherent Human Future," *Washington Post,* January 6, 2003.

Henry I. Miller, "Some Still Can't Digest Idea of Biotech Foods," *Investor's Business Daily,* April 15, 2004.

Henry I. Miller and Gregory Conko, "Technology's Unworthy Adversaries," *Hoover Digest,* Spring 2004.

James Pethokoukis, "Our Biotech Bodies, Ourselves," *U.S. News & World Report,* May 31, 2004.

Pew Initiative on Food and Biotechnology, "Feeding the World: A Look at Biotechnology and World Hunger," March 2004.

Jesse Reynolds, "Responding to Emerging Dangerous New Human Genetics," *Z Magazine,* April 2003.

Andrew Staehelin, "Genetically Modified Foods Safer than Organic," *Rocky Mountain News,* July 6, 2003.

Gregory Stock, "From Regenerative Medicine to Human Design: What Are We Really Afraid Of?" *Free Inquiry,* June/July 2004.

Wall Street Journal, "Genetic Food Fight," May 15, 2003.

World Watch, July/August 2002. Entire issue on genetic engineering.

Cathy Young, "Monkeying Around with the Self," Reason Online, April 2001.

Web Sites

Ag BioTech InfoNet (www.biotech-info.net). This site presents scientific reports and information on the use of biotechnology and genetic engineering in agriculture and food processing. It includes links to materials on the environmental and health effects of genetic engineering in agriculture, among other issues.

Betterhumans.com (www.betterhumans.com). This site explores and advocates the use of science and technology for furthering human progress. It supports the genetic engineering of humans, plants, and animals.

Genetically Engineered Organisms Public Issues Education Project (GEO-PIE) (www.geo-pie.cornell.edu/gmo.html). The GEO-PIE Project was developed to create objective educational materials exploring the complex scientific and social issues associated with genetic engineering in order to help readers consider those issues for themselves.

INDEX

European Union, 82, 86

fish, 95, 103–104
Fletcher, John, 52
Food and Drug Administration (FDA), 97–99, 103
Fox, Michael W., 104–105
Frankel, Mark S., 23
Frist, Bill, 90

Galton, Francis, 32
genetically modified (GM) crops, 77, 81, 97
  are not needed to feed the world, 68–69
  FDA regulation of, 97–99
  industry monopoly on, 90–92
  safety concerns about, are 72–74, 82–83
  con, 66, 97
genetic engineering, 65
  technique of, 44
  types of, 9–10
genetic enhancement. *See* germ line engineering
genetic screening, 25
  preimplantation and, 18
  technique of, 20
germ line, 21
germ line engineering, 9–10, 11, 24, 26

benefits of, 19, 21–22, 41–42, 52–53
  dangers of, 27–29, 34–36, 47, 49–51
  politics of, 20–21
  support for, 52–53
Gilder George, 58
GloFish, 104
Glover, Jonathan, 52
GM. *See* genetically modified crops
Greenpeace, 88

Hall, Tony, 88
Heinberg, Richard, 105
Hirsch, Karen, 100
Hughes, James, 50, 52
human genome, 55
human growth hormone (HGH), 27–28
humanity
  genetic reengineering will improve, 52–53, 59–62
human redesign. *See* germ line engineering
hunger, poverty is cause of, 86–87

India, 87, 90
inheritable genetic modification (IGM). *See* germ line engineering

somatic gene therapy, 9, 45

Stock, Gregory, 11, 15, 47, 50, 52

Technology Review (magazine), 16

Terminator technology, 68

Transhumanists, 53, 58

UN Food and Agriculture Organization (FAO), 89

United States, 90
    aid to Zambia from, 88

U.S. Agency for International Development (USAID), 90

Wambugu, Florence, 78, 79

Warwick, Kevin, 53

Watson, James, 51–52

Wondergenes: Genetic Enhancement and the Future of Society (Mehlman), 12

World Trade Organization (WHO), 86

Zambia, 79, 81–82
    U.S. aid to, 88

PICTURE CREDITS

ABOUT THE EDITOR

Scott Barbour received a bachelor's degree in English and a master's degree in social work from San Diego State University. He has worked as a case manager and counselor with the severely mentally ill. He is currently a senior acquisitions editor for Greenhaven Press, for whom he has edited numerous books on social issues, historical topics, and current events.